TREACY'S BRITISH RAIL

TREACY'S BRITISH RAIL

Patrick Whitehouse ARPS
and
John Powell CENG, FIMECHE

David & Charles

Endpapers: *front* The Railway Executive Timetable Map 1949; *back* British Railways Board Timetable Map 1965

Frontispiece: *One of Treacy's favourite locations, Edge Hill cutting, a spot which was not only dangerous but also only available for around six or so weeks a year. Most of these dramatic pictures must have been taken in mid summer and between 10.00 am and 11.00 am – the Merseyside Express was 10.00 am (later 10.10 am) from Liverpool Lime Street to Euston. This photograph was probably taken in the early to mid 1950s and shows a train headed by the usual class 7 4-6-0, normally a Royal Scot but on this occasion rebuilt Patriot (1948) No 45525 Colwyn Bay – an Edge Hill engine.*

A DAVID & CHARLES BOOK

Hardback edition first published 1990
Reprinted 1991
Paperback edition first published 2002

Copyright © Millbrook House Ltd, Patrick Whitehouse & John Powell 1990, 2002

Distributed in North America by F&W Publications, Inc.

A catalogue record for this book is available from the British Library.

ISBN 0 7153 9415 0 (hardback)
ISBN 0 7153 1380 0 (paperback)

Printed in China by
Hong Kong Graphics & Printing Ltd
for David & Charles
Brunel House   Newton Abbot   Devon

ACKNOWLEDGEMENTS

The authors would like to thank John Edgington of the National Railway Museum for his care, thoughtfulness and detective work not only in identifying many of the pictures but also picking out details of change and ensuring that these are properly described in the captions to them. In addition he has read through the text and kept us on the straight and narrow path through the jungle of dates and locomotive types and numbers. Eric Treacy was closely connected with the work of the Museum in his capacity as a Council Member of the Friends of The National Railway Museum, an appointment made by the Secretary of State.

The other member of the research team is John Smart who has spent many hours if not months searching through thousands of negatives identifying not only the motive power hardware but also important items of infrastructure many of which have been swept away during these days of modernisation and rationalisation. He and Jonathan Makepeace have made special journeys to obtain a number of 'comparative' photographs and we wish to record our appreciation of their help.

We are also grateful to Michael Harris, Managing Director of Ian Allan Ltd for allowing use of some of Eric Treacy's diary quotations from his early paperbacks in their *Best Railway Photographs* series and others from the introduction to their excellent hardbacks by Eric Treacy and, of course, from that magic *Steam Up*. These are clearly mentioned in the text and are indeed a vital part of the Eric Treacy story. Permission to quote the extract from the Bishop's biography *Eric Treacy* by J.S. Peart-Binns is acknowledged with thanks.

BIBLIOGRAPHY

My Best Railway Photographs	Eric Treacy	Ian Allan Ltd 1946
More of My Best Railway Photographs	Eric Treacy	Ian Allan Ltd 1947
Steam Up	Eric Treacy	Ian Allan Ltd 1949
The Lure of Steam	Eric Treacy	Ian Allan Ltd 1966
Eric Treacy	J.S. Peart-Binns	Ian Allan Ltd 1980
Fiennes on Rails	Gerard Fiennes	David & Charles 1986
BR Steam Motive Power Depots	Paul Bolger	Ian Allan Ltd 1984
Pictorial Record of BR Standard Steam Locomotives	E. Talbot	Oxford Publishing Co. 1982

CONTENTS

Getting ready for the road. A final oil round No 46240 City of Coventry. This photograph was taken prior to one of Eric Treacy's footplate trips on the down Royal Scot. The driver is R. (Dicky) Gray of Upperby shed.

City of Edinburgh No 6241 a Camden based Duchess class 4-6-2 shunts an extra coach for a southbound express at Carlisle Citadel on 11 April 1947. The locomotive is very dirty despite being de-streamlined and receiving the LMS 1946 black livery only a few months previously.

INTRODUCTION

Eric Treacy began his interest in photography during the 1930s. He was then vicar of Edge Hill, Liverpool, where many of his parishioners worked in the adjacent railway sheds and yards giving him a relationship with railways and railwaymen which was to last for the rest of his life. He was particularly proud to have these Edge Hill men numbered among his friends and some of them he got to know very well indeed. 'Farmer' Dick Georgson with his untidy moustache; George Shaw, all six feet of him with an excellent baritone voice; Beazley Foreshaw, always as clean and tidy at the end of a run as at the beginning, and many others including the renowned Laurie Earl the cheerful, tiny and ever smiling Cockney who was a star performer from London's Camden shed. As a natural development Treacy became part of the lives of the railwaymen he served and in turn he was a much loved pastor. Such a close contact enabled him to progress his hobby, wedding this to his interest in the railway itself as well as the men who worked on it. Some extracts from his 1947 diary clearly show his ongoing relationships, his easy way with people and his entering into a long and extremely successful period of professionalism as a railway photographer.

11th April. On Carlisle station I met Inspector Stanley Mead of Edge Hill, Liverpool, an old friend whom I have not seen since the beginning of the war. Turning our backs to the trains, we repaired to the Refreshment Room for lengthy draughts of tea. I heard all the news of shed 8A: then, finding he had an hour to spare before catching his train, I invited him to come and act as look-out man while I took some photographs. My prestige amongst lookers-on was greatly enhanced by the presence of the Inspectorial bowler hat. A good batch of photos resulted, including one of 6241 *City of Edinburgh*.

15th April. I have been to foregather with some old friends in the Penrith goods yard, who were greatly interested in my activities. It was their dinner hour, so I prevailed on them to provide human interest in the picture I intended to take of the 10am from Glasgow, a group was also taken. Unfortunately those good men are still waiting to see their photographs because the plates I used were, alas! stale and fogged, due to bad storing. I hate disappointing my friends on the railway. Herein is a warning: always store plates (and filters) in a cool dry place.

16th April. I visited Scout Green in the evening, and met once again Signalman Ratcliffe, who passes the time between trains with an enormous and high powered telescope – so powerful that he claims to be able to spot foxes on the Fells ten miles away. He was a sniper on the Somme in the 1914–18 war, and told me of a particularly good if gruesome 'hide' which he found for himself in a pile of dead in No Man's Land. He claims to have spent several profitable days amongst these pleasant surroundings! It was a beautiful evening, marred only by the sight of a large number of dead sheep on the Fells – the result of a severe winter. While here I got a picture of a 'Patriot' on a goods train, making very heavy weather of the gradient.

18th April. I nearly lost my life in the cause of railway photography

As a frequent visitor to Edge Hill shed Eric Treacy soon became acquainted with Stanier's Turbomotive No 6202, the Camden based engine's regular duty being the morning Euston – Liverpool express, returning in the early evening. This photograph, taken after rebuilding as a conventional 4-6-2 and becoming Princess Anne, *is one of Treacy's rare shots of the engine. It is waiting at Edge Hill to take the 5.25 pm 'Flyer' back to Euston in the late summer of 1952. He would have been grief stricken along with his railway friends at the Harrow disaster of 8 October 1952 when No 46202 was destroyed and 112 lives lost.*

The approach to Manchester London Road station in 1955. The incoming train is headed by a rebuilt Royal Scot: it is about to pass the departing 11.55 am to Kingswear and Plymouth (with three ex GWR coaches) behind Jubilee class 4-6-0 No 45644 Howe. The double headed train in the centre is the 12.05 pm to Euston via Stoke hauled by Jubilee No 45624 St Helena with a Fowler class 4 2-6-4T No 42399 as pilot to Stoke. The wires of two 1500v dc systems are visible, the Manchester South Junction and Altrincham on the left with class 4MT 4-6-0 No 75039 beneath them and the Manchester, Sheffield, Wath line on the right with electric class EM1 No 26033.

today, when a bottle thrown from a passing train missed my head by inches. This was criminal thoughtlessness on the part of some passenger. It should be drummed into the heads of the travelling public that over a stretch of 200 miles there will be as many as 1,000 permanent way men at work along the line, so that the chances of a flying bottle killing one of these men are pretty good – even if railway photographers' claims to existence are insignificant!

28th April. There was nearly a tragedy today. I am kind enough to allow my wife to use my basement dark room as a refrigerator for perishable goods. In the middle of developing some plates I was called away to the 'phone, during which time my wife slips in with the meat ration and in all innocence turns on the light; whereat 100 watts of light pour down on to my half developed plates for the space of one minute. I wrote them off as ruined: but then turned the light off again and put the plates into the hypo. Result – six perfect negatives, with not a sign of fog! I have yet to find anyone who can explain this apparent miracle. The plates were Kodak P.1200 and the developer, Johnson's Fine Grain, and although I don't recommend this method of development, I gave these facts on oath.

17th May. The double summer time has struck a grievous blow at railway photography in this part of the world. Here, the majority of the traffic is between 2 and 3pm which is midday by the sun. Consequently at the peak traffic period the sun is right overhead, giving very poor lighting and modelling. Further north or south, however,

D.B.S.T. must be a distinct advantage. In the summer months, the best time of the day for photographic lighting is before 10am and after 4pm.

16th June. I fell a victim today to my own lack of system. I carry my unused slides in the right hand pocket of my jacket and transfer them to the left pocket after exposure. I confess that my slides are never numbered and are quite indistinguishable one from the other. As I richly deserve, I got mixed up with my exposed and unexposed slides, with the result that I exposed one plate twice! I do recommend the careful numbering of each slide, and the recording in a note book of each picture as it is taken – and I do not advise carrying slides in pockets. I have learned my lesson!

28th June. A sweltering afternoon. The section of line I had chosen today runs beside a sewage farm, and – to be quite frank – it stank! Every train was a disappointment: the engines were filthy, the weather was too hot for exhaust, and there was a dreary lack of variety – one class 5 after another. But there came a hail from Scotty Boyle in the nearby signal box: "What about a cup of tea?" While the kettle boiled we chatted together and found that we were near neighbours in the Normandy battle for Caen. Before becoming a signalman he was a bus driver; now his only complaint about his present job was that ever-present sewage farm. Soon I was drinking as good a cup of tea as ever came out of a pot. Then with a roar there came into sight the 9.55am St Pancras to Glasgow and with a beautifully clean locomotive working hard and making much smoke. It was No 6133 *The Green Howards* a rebuilt 'Scot' on which much elbow grease had been expended.

As perhaps one would have expected Eric Treacy's approach to the railway was emotional rather than scientific or technical. In his first

Victoria station Chatham side. No 8 on the left is the arrival platform for boat trains with customs barriers in evidence. A number of these trains also departed from here but not the Night Ferry which normally left from platform 2. There is a continental train on the right with a motor luggage van at its head; these used battery power at Dover and Folkestone to run from the end of the third rail to the ship loading points.

Kings Cross departure side, platforms 6 to 10 (except 9) with two up arrivals. Unloading at platform 8 is the 06.30 Cleethorpes–Kings Cross express composed of MkI stock and hauled by a class 37. The Pullman cars of the Master Cutler are in platform 6. The date is about 1964 after steam had been banished from Kings Cross. The crowds gathering on platform 10 may well be for the Flying Scotsman.

hardback book (some say his best) entitled *Steam Up* one chapter is headed 'For Pleasure' and its first line asks "Whose?" with the answer, "Mostly mine!!" He made it clear that its preparation (and that went for all his books) provided a joyful relaxation enabling him to share his enthusiasm with so many others. Always he was concerned with the atmosphere of HIS railway – not the rambling branch line or the struggling narrow gauge – it was the attack on Shap Fell or Ais Gill, the vista from Durham station on an autumn morning looking out over smoking chimneys to the great mass of the cathedral, trains departing from Liverpool Lime Street and climbing through the smoky cuttings, from Euston up Camden bank and, when, as an archdeacon, he visited Lambeth Palace a quick nip out to Victoria, Waterloo or even Paddington. Without question the Duchess Pacifics held the Treacy crown but any engine exuding power and personality would have his rapt attention. The spell of the railway seemed to pick him up and raise his spirits, the swig of tea on the footplate of a Royal Scot running from Leeds to Carlisle, the sulphurous smell of an engine shed, all this smelling and seeing and hearing somehow had to be recorded on film. Sometimes he would say that he was guilty of overdoing his Shap and Beattock pictures but his aim was perfection and there could be no better spots than these for his purpose. Here there could be everything he needed if his luck was in, the hard working steam engines (one of the epitomies of power should it be a Duchess) the wild moorland scenery, magnificent cloud effects: all the pieces of the jigsaw needed to turn a photograph into a painting. Treacy never tired of the search both for the idyllic railway memory or an attempt to obtain that master shot. In *Steam Up*, his mind on a scene not far from that beloved Shap Fell he wrote:–

What more charming than the country station where seemingly little ever happens, and the arrival of a train is something of an event. Stations where the station master doesn't wear a top hat, but has time to talk, and is often to be found in his shirt sleeves tending the station garden or feeding his hens. I remember spending a very happy afternoon one holiday, on a station in Cumberland between Carlisle and Penrith. The sun shone out of a blue sky; a small beck gurgled under a bridge at the end of the platform; in the station yard the local youngsters were playing Red Indians and Cowboys; in the adjacent fields the cattle made those deep-throated noises peculiar to cattle; the signalman sat on the steps of his box reading a newspaper; the porter was doing a bit of gardening; and in the booking office a kettle was boiling on the gas ring in preparation for the afternoon cup of tea. Above, the larks sang: below, the crickets chirped. Then into this idyllic scene there comes the imperious ring of the signal bell. The signalman drops his paper, a good deal more ringing takes place; then one by one the signal arms drop. Subtly, the whole atmosphere has changed. I sit up on my seat and rub the sleep out of my eyes; the Cowboys and Indians sign an armistice and come and stand expectantly on the platform; the porter drops his trowel and starts to sweep the platform. Even the cattle start to eye the line with a bleary interest. Old men gardening in the nearby village, farm labourers, the postman, the village policeman, a host of people

The railway scene at Tebay around 1960 showing Jubilee class 4-6-0 No 45717 Dauntless heading south through the station with a Liverpool bound express. Rising above the second coach is Tebay No 2 box with the ex North Eastern Railway branch to Kirkby Stephen running off to the right: this used a separate platform and had its own shed facilities. To the left of the picture is the old LNWR shed (12H in May 1960) used for the Shap bankers.

previously invisible appear at a variety of vantage points along the line – sitting on gates, looking over bridges, leaning against fences. All seems set for something really big to happen; and in a flash it does happen. The 'Coronation Scot' gleaming in the sunshine framed momentarily in the arch of a bridge, hurls itself through the station. We get an impression rather than a view – of smoke, gleaming paint, throbbing movement; and while we are trying to sort out our impressions into their chronological order, the train is gone.

Then follows a certain anti-climax. For the village the big event of the day was come and gone. Slowly the scene reverts to its earlier peace – the more so because somebody now has taken the kettle off and made a pot of tea. Like a motion picture that has been stopped and then started again, all the characters in the scene start doing again what they were doing when this steaming Hercules burst in upon them. The signalman picks up his paper, the porter gets back to his roses, the kids start scrapping again, the cattle resume munching. One is conscious again of the gurgle of the running water and of the larks above who have continued to sing in spite of the interruption below. The strollers from the village, having timed their stroll nicely, continue to stroll. And I tilt my hat over my nose and am relaxing once again on the hard station seat when there comes the sort of friendly call that is so typical of the country and its kindness – "What about a cup of tea, mister?" Yes, these country stations have a charm all their own. Part of the charm is that they aren't as blasé as the big stations. The 'Flying Hamburger' could pass through Crewe or York without anyone appearing to notice it: but in the country they know how to be excited. They are capable of appreciating things that ought to be appreciated. And they don't worry about platform tickets!

By the middle 1960s Eric Treacy had been taking railway photographs for a third of a century and would sometimes joke that he was 'rather a period piece', though it would have been both unwise and untrue to say that to him face to face. In fact he kept himself young in spite of not being blessed with children, being happy to mix with people of all ages, emphasising that although he had what was popularly regarded as an odd hobby he was in all other respects normal. *Who's Who* actually listed his hobby as 'pottering about locomotive sheds'. In one of his pictorial books *Lure of Steam* Treacy admitted that as his score in years was increasing he tended to look backward rather than forward, with memories becoming increasingly precious and his ability to adjust to change more difficult, but in these thoughts he was much influenced by the impending demise of the things he loved. No longer could he stroll down No 1 platform at Paddington to hear the curiously rude noises peculiar to Great Western engines or the thunder of an un-rebuilt 'Royal Scot' blasting its way up the 1 in 95 from Liverpool's Lime Street station to Edge Hill – a sound which literally shook his vicarage at Liverpool. Nor could he watch the pillars of smoke rising skyward at York as the great Pacifics slipped and struggled to get their trains moving from the platforms and round the north curve.

Not that Treacy was a sentimentalist – far from it – his realism, for

Eric Treacy's ability to mix with people and to obtain the friendship and trust of railwaymen stood him in good stead as this fascinating picture shows. Tebay No 2 was a modern LMS style signalbox with many comforts denied to brother signalmen elsewhere, hot water and electric light being two examples. The box controlled the junction with the ex NER branch, the intermediate block signals at Tebay North and the entrance to the locomotive yard. The frame was the standard LMS type with shortened lever tops for colour-light signals and ex LNWR type instruments. The shed lines (bottom of diagram) and branch exit (top) are clearly shown. The Kirkby Stephen branch closed in 1962 with station and shed going in 1968.

example, demanded that he should give up his living as vicar of Edge Hill and join the armed forces to help safeguard the then last bastion of the free world against Nazi-ism. He never forgot those times, as his earlier diary comments have shown. He was a lively debater when politics entered into the scene, as they often did during his ministries, and he readily acknowledged the logic and realism of motive power design as being 'a contrast between sleek efficiency and belching, gorgeous inefficiency' with the railway reflecting actual changes in society. His throw away comment was that if there had to be diesel electric locomotives then the Deltic was about the best one could get! One reason why he took pictures of every single member of the class. But those memories were always there and what is more they were backed up by well over 10,000 superb negatives.

No wonder *Portrait of Steam* came out in 1967, *Glory of Steam* in 1969 and *Roaming the Northern Rails* (his last book) in 1976: shortly before his death he was contemplating the biggest block buster of all with two tone separations for his black and white pictures and the cream of those too – it was to have been a tremendous swan song.

Most of Eric Treacy's pictures were taken in the post World War II era with the real volume coming in the 1950s and early 1960s. Though because of his calling (which gave him neither enough time nor money to do as he would have wished with his railway photography) his photographs are somewhat limited in their locations. Even so, few opportunities were lost – for example he was able to make a good deal

Eric Treacy had many authorised, semi authorised and unofficial footplate trips when he always took his camera. This shot was almost certainly taken on the northbound North Briton with the crew of A2/2 No 60501 Cock o' the North as his hosts. The photograph shows driver Ingelson in the usual stance of a man used to full regulator working.

of the old Midland main line when Rector of Keighley, and this gave him the chance to record that superb piece of railway in the heyday of rebuilt Royal Scots and Jubilees as well as being within a two hour car journey of his beloved Shap Fell. On his days off he would happily head north to the wild country, often taking the opportunity of a footplate ride readily granted by the railway authorities (usually locally and not necessarily officially) – and how he enjoyed *that*: having a go with the shovel, sharing the billy can of tea and getting to know the crews from Holbeck and Kingmoor. Other footplate trips included the run from Leeds to Newcastle, often on the North Briton, with Neville Hill men to York. Some of his finest pictures of people were taken on these footplates where he was able to catch that almost inexplicable atmosphere of men and machines working together.

After he became an archdeacon there were periodic visits to London and Treacy never tired of telling stories of how he made friends with the stationmaster at Euston, Harry Turrell, who would make arrangements for him to be accompanied to Camden Bank – often coming himself – top hat and all. But his greater delight was to be able to recall the more officious and less helpful attitudes he received at Kings Cross and how he managed (like so many other photographers of note) to obtain welcomes from signalmen around Gas Works and Copenhagen tunnels as well as at the Top Shed. Eric Treacy was nothing if not a human being.

As Bishop of Wakefield it was not so easy for Treacy to maintain the common touch, though his human-ness allowed him to dig himself further into both (as he would put it) the vertical and horizontal scenes. Geoff Bird who was shed master at York in the later days of steam and Ronnie Taylor the district motive power superintendent at Leeds were each able to hold a number of doors ajar for him. Ronnie Taylor would accompany the Railway Bishop on the footplate of one of his favourite rebuilt Scots over the Settle–Carlisle line giving Treacy turns on the shovel whilst he took the regulator – something that spells out the human relationships which both men could achieve, for the driver is always in charge of his engine and if he said no to this very unofficial and un-Bishoplike arrangement then it would have *been* no. There must have been some lively and witty exchanges, for Treacy was a great lover of ex LMS engines (his early days at Edge Hill ensured that) whilst Taylor was an ex Darlington apprentice.

Geoff Bird, ex Darlington apprentice and a fellow enthusiast for steam (as far as he could be seen to be in those difficult days of BR) came to York as shed master, relieving another old friend of Eric Treacy's, Lawrence Reeves, in August 1965. He found a number of residual steam locomotives (among them some A1 Pacifics including No 60145 *St Mungo*, various V2s, No 60866 the last LNER steam engine to haul a Royal Train plus a variety of B1s and K1s for local workings) mixed in with a fleet of class 40 and class 20 diesel electrics. At that time Centralised Locomotive Control had not yet come into force and the allocation of engines to turns of duty was very much in the hands of the Running Foreman whose decision was sometimes influenced by the Mechanical Foreman for technical reasons and occasionally by the Shed Master for other reasons. Needless to say these 'other reasons' usually provided a flurry of eager railway photographers when certain locomotives appeared on particular turns. One of these

Treacy's crown was always awarded to Stanier's Duchess Pacifics and a footplate ride on one of those superb machines working the Royal Scot was something to be more than savoured. This photograph taken at Euston in the mid to late 1950s was Treacy's caring gift for the loco crew and his friend Harry Turrell the stationmaster here arrayed in all his glory. The driver (shown earlier on shed) is R. (Dicky) Gray, the fireman D. Moffat both of Upperby whilst the inspector (specially provided to accompany him) is Sam F. Smith of Rugby.

was the Sunderland Mail (3G13) which left York at 0330 via the coast running as a class A train to Stockton working back from Heaton over the main line to York and then on to Manchester as 3M50. This was headed for a while by A1 Pacifics and V2s and after their demise by most of the Holbeck Jubilees. One may well ask how the Jubilees got in on the act over the NE main line. The fact was that for reasons Geoff Bird feels better not pursued 3M30 required a steam engine on certain occasions and the B1s left at York shed would not keep time on the main line with loads approaching those on 3M30.

Whilst all this was going on it takes little imagination to appreciate that a frequent visitor to York shed was a certain Bishop. He called in to introduce himself to Geoff Bird, had a chat, took a few pictures, talked to the men and then popped off. His visits usually coincided with a summons which he had received from Higher Authority – to whom he referred as the CO. Dr Coggan was the Archbishop of York at the time and it is not altogether surprising to find that he had a number of footplate trips from York on the 0800 to Kings Cross on a class 47. Reading between the lines it all goes to prove that the Bishop of Wakefield was not only thoughtful towards his superiors but very much a human being.

Also returning to this story is Eric Treacy's friend Ronnie Taylor and his strange conversion. Taylor as we know was another Darlington

Polmadie Pacifics at Carlisle. The down Royal Scot is headed by Duchess 4-6-2 No 46224 Princess Alexandra *whilst BR standard class 6 4-6-2 No 72006* Clan Mackenzie *waits in the adjacent road to take over the Perth portion of the train. Note that the Duchess is in reverse gear having set back to loosen the couplings. No 46224 still carries the flattened smokebox top, a legacy of its streamlined days, this also helps to date the picture to between 1953 and 1954 when the smokebox was rebuilt.*

A morning in 1960 showing class 31 No D5589 on an empty stock train from either the terminus or Moorgate; it is brand new and carries neither a yellow warning panel nor electrification warning flashes. On the right is the original A4 Pacific No 60014 Silver Link waiting to come off Top Shed prior to working the down Flying Scotsman.

Like many other enthusiasts Treacy was deeply impressed by the beautiful curve of York station. This October 1956 view shows an up express standing in platform 8, with a Peppercorn class A1 Pacific opposite at Platform 9 apparently heading an empty stock train. Note the smartly dressed passengers, the gas lighting and the entwined initials NER in the spandrel supporting the signal on the left.

apprentice and one who having spent most of his life on the North Eastern until his translation from HQ at York had been avid in his respect for their products; he considered all things LMS a load of rubbish including their engines. Be that as it may, he had only been District Motive Power Superintendent at Leeds – with Holbeck and the S&C under his wing – for a short time when he suddenly changed his partisanship towards LMS locomotives, not all of them but certainly to the mainstays of the Holbeck fleet; Royal Scots, Jubilees, Black Fives and the Class 8s. In the still ensconced bastions of NE territory they could hardly believe their ears. Thus with Ronnie Taylor as his companion those Eric Treacy rides over S&C and other fortuitous happenings were true delight in a very late Indian summer. The romance of the footplate and of steam engines in general was a most consuming affair in the lives of certain professional railwaymen and of an unusual and cared for Bishop.

Geoff Bird remembers Eric Treacy as a man who was able to endear himself to the rank and file of railwaymen much the same way as the human and highly respected railway General Manager Gerard Fiennes. The secret was to understand their jobs, know how they were done and appreciate the value of that job to the industry. This Treacy did very well at York and in his excursions to the shed he would engage some unsuspecting man in discussion about this or that who, at the sight of his dog collar would be completely disarmed. Of course in his various expeditions it always went down very well if a certain amount of skill or otherwise was demonstrated with the shovel. It was not completely unknown for him to visit his CO with dirty hands.

As steam on the national railway system died it resurrected itself in preservation and tourism, and although the Bishop made noises to the effect that he was going to move over to gardening and walking once he could no longer hear the thunder of steam on Shap – of course it never happened. One of his first entries into this new field was his election as president of the Keighley & Worth Valley Railway right on his doorstep. Here he was able to offer statesmanship combined with a love of both the hardware and the people concerned.

A little nearer to home as far as this author is concerned Eric Treacy also took an interest in the slow but steady growth of the Birmingham Railway Museum. He had known Geoff Bird so well in the late 1960s that he could pop in and out of York shed almost at will and when ex Western Region, but then privately owned, No 7029 *Clun Castle* came to York for trials prior to running over the east coast main line in the late spring of 1967 both men were bubbling over with excitement. The runs, arranged by that ebullient general manager at Liverpool Street, Gerry Fiennes, and supervised by the enthusiastic and experienced Richard Hardy, were a tremendous success and led to the private purchase of No 5593 *Kolhapur* based at Holbeck. Eric Treacy was over the moon – this was an engine that finished its working life running turns over *his* Settle–Carlisle route. As both engines were based on Birmingham friendships developed and refined leaving an unfillable hole when Treacy died only relieved by the surety that here was a Man of God who really was God's Man.

But there was another connection with Birmingham. Two other pioneers in the field of serious railway preservation Brian Hollingsworth and Geoffrey Drury, had purchased an ex LMS Black

The NER spandrel (shown opposite) is still in situ although now devoid of its colour-light head. (John Edgington)

17

Five No 5428 (also a Leeds Holbeck engine) and were then keeping it at Tyseley. They asked Treacy if he would consent to their naming the locomotive *Bishop of Wakefield* – it was descended via Sir William Stanier from a long line of Great Western Railway named engines going back to the Saints of early Edwardian days and an ecclesiastical name was more than appropriate. What better than to acknowledge the feelings of so many people for the 'Railway Bishop'. Treacy, human as always, asked if the name could be more specific, as there were several other Bishops of Wakefield still living; so No 5428 became *Eric Treacy*.

The ceremony took place on a fine spring day in 1969, 3 May to be exact, and this recorded two firsts – the first member of the Bishop class and the first such naming ceremony to be performed by a Bishop – in this instance Leonard Wilson, the then Bishop of Birmingham, another much loved and highly respected cleric. Wilson had spent much of World War II as a prisoner of the Japanese having been taken captive when he was Bishop of Singapore; his bravery and constant help to other prisoners made him something of a national hero remembered by many for his conducting the annual Festival of Remembrance services at the Albert Hall. He was, of course, a member of the British Legion; in addition and very fitting for the occasion he was also a Bradshaw addict who collected and studied railway timetables. It was fortunate that not only did he know Treacy well but also had a link with the owners of the other preserved engines at Tyseley. After smashing the ceremonial bottle of champagne on a crosshead, No 5428 was well and truly christened, with the two bishops duly climbing on to the footplate as soon as the deed was done. A memorable occasion which is still treasured by everyone who was privileged to be there.

This ceremony helped to cement a strong friendship and Eric Treacy was able to add yet another railway link to his chain. Another happening in Birmingham also helped to show Eric Treacy's human side. He was guest of honour at the prestigious Grand Junction Club, a select dining affair limited to thirty people whose interest is not just railways but good fellowship and good food. Naturally the visit meant a trip down to Tyseley to see the engines but Treacy was apt to travel casually when on pleasure and did not wear his dog collar in the earlier

Eric Treacy was President of the Keighley and Worth Valley Railway, a position he greatly valued and one where he was able to use his talents of communication to advantage. So it is not surprising that Evening Star *made its first visit to a private tourist line a Yorkshire one. The scene here is Mytholmes viaduct with a Keighley–Oxenhope train. The engine was actually borrowed from the NRM in July 1973 prior to the opening of the museum in 1975.*

No 7029 Clun Castle inside York North shed in the summer of 1967. The locomotive was undergoing clearance trials over the ECML prior to running a series of steam specials. Although No 7029 was a BR built Castle (1950) it was then painted in GWR guise as BR did not wish to have a preserved locomotive running in its livery. Behind is one of the later series of class 20s built with four character route indicator panels in place of disc headcodes.

part of the day – in fact he forgot to bring it at all though he did remember his purple stock. There was some consternation for a while but the author's wife found a large brand new and starched table napkin and we pinned it all up for him. Treacy was not only thankful but highly amused and no one appeared to notice.

One of the highlights of the 1970s was the 150th anniversary celebrations of the Stockton & Darlington Railway and needless to say Eric Treacy was there with his camera. There was a fully televised church service on 17 August at Bank Top station where he gave an address from a locomotive tender but some of his railway photographic friends remember a more personal occasion when Treacy was looking for a good vantage point from which to take his pictures. One obvious place was at the top of a none too solid fire escape serving the offices and this became somewhat overloaded. Matters were made worse when yet another well known and equally well loved railway cleric, the late Reverend Teddy Boston, turned up. Teddy was no light weight and Treacy was heard to offer to 'pull rank' and order him off. Both got their pictures and Teddy Boston dined out on this story for many a day. J.S. Peart-Binns in his biography of *Treacy the Man* quotes many more examples of how the subject of his book endeared himself to church and lay folk alike.

Maybe Treacy was a bit of a soft touch for those who wanted him to grace their enterprises or become a welcome speaker but it must be said that he enjoyed these occasions as much as those who asked him. Not that everyone got off lightly for these speeches and talks were

19

No 5428 Eric Treacy stands in Tyseley yard on 3 May 1969 after being named by Leonard Wilson, the Bishop of Birmingham. The engine had just been repainted in LMS colours at Birmingham Railway Museum. The photograph shows the Tyseley scene as it was immediately after the demolition of the roundhouse (1968) and prior to the site's re-development as a railway museum. On the left is the loco depot's diesel crane used for coaling the odd steam engine which until 1968 came into the diesel depot for wheel turning.

always thought out thoroughly and sometimes there were warnings given regarding enthusiast behaviour and responsibility well sprinkled with anecdotes to ensure that the points went home.

Another link with all those concerned professionally or otherwise on the railway scene was Treacy's position as a nominee (on behalf of the Secretary of State) on the Council of the Friends of the National Railway Museum from March 1978. This gave him the opportunity to feel that he had a hand in the preservation of vital artefacts belonging to our railway system whilst being in a position of great responsibility which he took very much to heart.

Little has been said here about the nuts and bolts of Eric Treacy's photography but this has been covered in some detail elsewhere both in his own writings and by Dr John Coiley, Keeper to the National Railway Museum in his introduction to the Bishop's memorial book by this publisher *Eric Treacy – Railway Photographer*. Nevertheless it is well worth remembering that he started off his hobby, as with everything else, by giving it considerable thought, even though he was only in his 20s and running a large boys' club in the Liverpool dockside. Not for him the Box Brownie but a tool which would do the job right – a Leica later running the gamut that so many railway photographers ran by moving to ¼ plate glass (and what superb negatives those Soho Reflex and Zeiss Contessa Press cameras produced though it is worth remembering that they were made for the professionals and did not come cheaply, a good Zeiss Contessa, Nettel Minimum Palmos or Thornton Pickard could cost up to £40 second hand – a vast amount of money in those days; one reason for the comparative paucity of good railway photographers in the old days) to Rolleiflex and Super Ikonta cameras though never disposing of this faithful Leica which he used often for his later BR shots. Whatever technical reappraisal Eric Treacy was to encounter the quality of his pictures never wavered.

He set himself a number of basic rules:–

The naming ceremony for ex LMS class 5P5F 4-6-0 No 5428 at Tyseley BR locomotive depot on 3 May 1969. On the left is the Bishop of Birmingham, Leonard Wilson, and on the right the Bishop of Wakefield, Eric Treacy: each in his own right an enthusiast for railway subjects. Bishop Wilson was a Bradshaw addict, Bishop Treacy one of Britain's finest railway photographers. (Birmingham Post & Mail)

1 To take his photographs only in proper lighting conditions – putting his camera away from November till March. There were of course a few exceptions where the occasional breach was vital, for example the picture reproduced later in this book of *Belgian Marine* toiling up Shap on a wet and windy day. But that was during the 1948 locomotive exchanges and it was then or never. As time went on and steam (along with other aspects of the railway scene) was disappearing fast this section of the rules was to become less operative.

2 To use his imagination in composing his pictures and planning ahead, always on the watch for new locomotives in the limited locations he was able to visit due to his calling, family life and the unavailability of unlimited money.

3 To make every exposure count.

4 To standardise on plates and developers to ensure that he had a constant and consistent knowledge of how emulsions behave in given circumstances. And ALWAYS to do the job himself. Treacy could be scathing in his criticism of those whom he termed 'button pushers' who merely purchased their film, took photographs and used outside processors.

Looking through thousands of his prints, well developed (and equally important) properly fixed, it would, using the materials available at the time, have been hard to improve them. Today using modern paper his negatives print even better.

In spite of Treacy's regret at the passing of steam he made his views that the railway must progress prominent enough in his writing though these were tinged with regret for days past. In *Lure of Steam* he wrote

The new railways which are taking shape may be economically more viable, operationally more efficient, but I doubt whether they

G. Parkin, British Railways Shildon yard manager takes a last look at LNWR Precedent class 2-4-0 No 790 Hardwicke before it moves off to take part in the great parade of engines celebrating the 150th anniversary of the opening of the Stockton & Darlington Railway on 31 August 1975.
Eric Treacy preached from the tender of one of the locomotives and was thus able to couple his pastoral duties with his determination to be present at this historic event.

will endear themselves to the public nor will they inspire the emotional attachment in the same way, or to the same extent as did the railway in the days of coal and water combining together to produce steam.

Three years later in *The Glory of Steam* he wrote

No longer do we see the driver and his mate mooching round the streets of our cities in between runs, their rations in an old respirator case, their overalls and headgear being an unmistakable uniform – all this has gone, and we are the poorer for it. The modern driver is clean, and to my ageing eyes, astonishingly youthful; at the end of the day he melts into the crowd of hurrying passengers: but make no mistake, he is playing his full part in the creation of a superb railway system. No, we must not so give ourselves up to sentimentality and nostalgia that we fail to see how well footplate staff have been in accepting the great change over. We rejoice in the much more comfortable conditions that they now enjoy and at the same time recognise them as the true descendents of those splendid railwaymen who raced from London to Aberdeen, who did their splendid 'bit' in the two great wars, and whose weather beaten and cheerful faces we no longer see stuck out of the cab side as they bring their trains safely to their journey's end.

These words were penned over twenty years ago and the majority of today's generation of footplatemen know little of the detailed handling of the great beast of steam though a remarkably large number are not only active on the tourist lines but seek to ensure their place on the steam links still in force to run main line specials over large stretches of country. Sadly Eric Treacy was unable to take many of the pictures that he would have liked, for most of these steam specials run on a Sunday, a day naturally kept for his calling and his duty. But this did not diminish his interest or his enthusiasm. Diesels were not so easy to photograph but Eric Treacy made the very best he could of the job and today some of these photographs are priceless in that they show scenes almost unrecognisable with artefacts and trains running where there is now a railway desert. So much so that it has been decided to add a few non Treacy pictures to the book just to make those stark comparisons.

A side light on just how Eric Treacy could bring life to an event is evident by the slightly differing views of a railway happening. In *Eric Treacy* by J.S. Peart-Binns the author refers to a diary extract.

Garsdale sometime in the mid 1950s and a then typical railway scene little known today, telegraph poles, ex Midland semaphore signals, fencing and oil lamps plus the junction to Hawes whence it made an end on meet with the ex NER branch from Northallerton. The view has been taken from the signalbox steps and shows a Glasgow bound express behind a rebuilt Royal Scot class 4-6-0 No 46112 Sherwood Forester. The stockaded turntable can be seen behind the telegraph poles and beyond this the arches of Dandry Mire viaduct.

3 February 1968. Great fun this afternoon. Gerard Fiennes (ex Manager, Eastern Region, BR) and I named a steam locomotive *Matthew Murray* in the Middleton Railway Yards near Hunslet, Leeds. I named it *Matthew* and he named it *Murray*, after which we pulled a string so violently that we not only revealed the nameplate but very nearly pulled the engine over on top of us. We then mounted the footplate, and I drove the engine like the 'Titfield Thunderbolt' down some fairly rough track towards a brick wall. We were romping happily along, making some 10mph, when I realised, I didn't know where the steam brake was. Visions

An extremely filthy class 5 4-6-0 is coupled in behind class 45 diesel electric No D28 on 1M86 the up Thames–Clyde Express as it approaches Dent around 1967. The steam engine is probably coupled into the train because of a failure of the diesel's train heating boiler.

of Bishop charging through brick wall into the thick of the Leeds traffic! However with seconds to spare I found it, and gave it all I had got with the result that we came to a standstill in our own length, nearly throwing Gerry Fiennes off the footplate. We did two or three runs for the benefit of photographers and tape recordists, and left *Matthew Murray* gently simmering in the January sunshine. A very good time had by all!

But the other participant, a lively and highly respected extrovert senior railwayman saw it slightly differently. In his last book *Fiennes on Rails* the late Gerard Fiennes wrote a tailpiece which he entitled *all This And, Nearly, Heaven Too*

"Bishop, for God's sake, put on that brake!!"

Not many of you have had the opportunity or the need to speak so sharply to a prelate. Indeed it would be a surprise if anyone reading this had ever been firemen to a bishop. But if anyone has, then, so to speak, this bishop was certainly *that* bishop. Eric Treacy no less.

He and I had been invited to perform a ceremony on the Middleton Railway. The most dramatic part was to embark on *Matthew Murray* and drive it for the entertainment of a crowd of well-wishers who, when the thing went wrong, were visibly and audibly sorry that it had not gone crashingly wrong.

We paraded. We embarked. "Will you drive?" said Eric. I had seen that the fire was well up and bright. So I said: "No, I'll do the firing" and leant in a negligent attitude on the corner of the cab.

"Right" said Eric. He pulled the whistle cord deafeningly and jerked at the regulator.

We shot off backwards, neither of us having observed that *Matthew* was in reverse gear. And that would not have been so bad if fifty yards away the points had not been set for a siding. Immediately inside it stood a wagon loaded with very solid projecting steel. So . . .

"Bishop, for God's sake put on that brake!!"

Eric laughed all over his face, being maybe more ready to meet his Headquarters upstairs than was a railway general manager. He reached for the nearest thing and jerked. A deafening whistle again. The next handle was the right one. We slid to a shrieking halt a few yards clear.

Perhaps it is apt to end this introduction with Treacy's view of the *Spell of the Railway* taken from *Steam Up*. It was written just before the era taken in by this book but its message covered those fascinating years when steam was in its Indian Summer.

The Spell of the Railway is made up of so many things which through the years have imprinted themselves on one's memory. Like Wordsworth's Daffodils:

> "they flash upon that inward eye . . .
> then my heart with pleasure fills."

One of the locations to appear again and again among the Treacy negatives is Edinburgh Waverley – and not without reason for this was a superb station with excellent photographic opportunities. The picture shows Waverley in 1960 with class A4 No 60009 Union of South Africa *(now preserved) of Haymarket shed waiting to take over an up express and class 26 diesel electric No D5305 probably on the relative empty stock. Note the use of both disc and lamp on D5305 which has only just arrived in Scotland having originally been allocated to the Eastern Region.*

A more unusual Waverley picture taken in the East End box showing three signalmen and a booking boy. This was replaced in 1981 by a new Waverley signalling centre but at that time it controlled all trains out of the east end of the station. On the top left are the gradient profiles for the respective routes, those for Drem Junction (main line), Piershill loop via Lochend being clearly visible in the centre. The date is 1954–5.

One of the Holbeck Jubilee class 4-6-0s, No 45577 Queensland *runs through Dent station with the down Thames–Clyde Express sometime during the late 1950s. The photograph is dated by the use of 'blood and custard' and maroon stock. The station buildings are still in good order and the platforms well kept but the snow fences are showing signs of a lack of maintenance.*

For me, the spell began with those holiday journeys from Liverpool to Penrith, with the sight of the first stone wall between Carnforth and Oxenholme: the distant Lakeland hills as the train began the climb up to Shap – that lovely but sometimes sombre cutting at Dillicar: then the slogging climb to Shap summit, what time the engine's beat became indignantly emphatic, and the grazing sheep on the Fell fled to quieter pastures. A glimpse, perhaps, into that lonely one man box at Scout Green – other glimpses into farmyards in which man and beast seemed to be momentarily transfixed.

The spell – it's the friendly noise of shunting during the long and wakeful hours of the night: and it is the noise of coal being broken in the tender as the engine awaits its job. It's the fussy little 'Cauliflower' making its shaky way from Penrith to Keswick and it's the gleaming monster bringing its 500 tons into King's Cross. It's the sight of signal lights winking and gleaming on a winter's evening: it's the orange light of the fire reflected on the billowing steam of the engine at night. It's the deafening noise of an engine blowing off in a station: it's the sound of carriage doors being slammed: it's the noise of milk churns being trundled, of eerie whistles in the night, of a signal bell tinkling in a nearby box, of the heavy thud of a signal lever being operated.

Dent station on 15 October 1988 with a Birmingham–Carlisle charter special passing through; it consists of two Derby built class 115 four car units allocated to Tyseley and more at home on the Birmingham suburban services. The station buildings are now privately owned and all is still neat and tidy though the snow fence has deteriorated even further. The signal box, sidings and the traditional signalling have all gone. Dent station was closed in May 1970 but reopened again in 1987. (J. Makepeace)

An unidentified class 45 approaches
Ais Gill summit with a southbound
partially fitted freight for the Eastern
Region c1970. Apart from
repainting into blue livery the 1Co-
Co1 is in original condition. All the
class 45s were later fitted with dual
brakes.

Except for the different locomotive
class the photograph of No 47540
shows very little change when
compared with the shot of eighteen
years back. The signal immediately
in front of the bridge disappeared
when Ais Gill box was closed. By
the end of 1988 only passenger
trains used the Settle–Carlisle route;
a typical example is illustrated here
with class 47 Co-Co No 47540
heading early MkII stock on the
16.40 Carlisle–Leeds on 14 October
1988. (J. Makepeace)

A photograph almost reminiscent of
the epic Southern Railway poster
taken at Leeds Central station
around 1956. The guard checks the
train loading and other required
running details with the locomotive
crew led by the renowned Bill Hoole
– note the driver's nameplate to the
left of the fireman's hand, a short
lived experiment. The engine is one
of Gresley's A4 class Pacifics No
60034 Lord Faringdon. It was
originally named Peregrine but was
renamed in March 1948.

It's the sight of a plume of steam away down in the valley as you stand on some hillside like Pen-y-Ghent watching a train on its way: the torture of standing on Euston platform on a hot summer's day with your own holiday past, and watching a train pull out marked LONDON–HOLYHEAD; and as you watch you think of the lovely ruins of Chester, the mountains of North Wales, and the golden sands of the Welsh Coast – and as you stand, you pine. It's the excitement of meeting someone you love on a railway station: of deciding where you will stand when the train draws in: of how you will greet them: of trying to anticipate what they will look like. It's the misery of separation too, as a train draws out carrying someone away whose company is perfect happiness – and whose absence is utter gloom. It's that Tea Room in Euston where they make the loveliest China Tea anywhere in England: it's the swig of cold tea on the footplate of a rebuilt Scot that has laboured up the hill to Blea Moor on the way from Leeds to Carlisle, when engine and crew relax with the prospect of several miles easy running. The fireman mops his brow: the driver looks at his watch, and grins when he finds that he has done it with two minutes to spare – and out comes the bottle of tea.

And it's the sulphurous smell of an engine shed: it's the fishy smell of a guard's van: it's the oily smell of the porter's room: the hot smell of an engine at the end of its journey. It's the whiff of ozone which comes through the open window of your carriage as the train approaches the sea: the smell of cut grass as you pass through the farmlands of England. It's the fun of knowing a bit more about the workings of the railway than the other people in your carriage – the fun of waving to pretty girls from a moving train knowing that it is quite safe!

Seeing, smelling and hearing – thus come our memories and impressions: thus is the spell created, and thus maintained. The Railway isn't just a thing which exists for our convenience. It is a world into which we enter for the time of our journeying. It is a world peopled with clearly defined types – a world with its own traditions and way of doing things: a world in which there is a strong camaraderie, which is by no means closed to those not of it who are prepared to appreciate it and learn more about it.

No one could have put it better.

One of Eric Treacy's regular photographic spots was the signalbox at Wortley Junction Leeds, on the right of the picture. Walking to and fro he often came into contact with local railwaymen including this trackgang. Note the men have no high visibility vests and the look out man with his standard issue of flags and horn. The six tracks here include two ex North Eastern to the left and four Midland on the right.

THE INTERCHANGE TRIALS OF 1948

The ghillie, pedalling south in the rain on the A9 to his cottage at Dalnacardoch, and with his mind on the Glorious Twelfth, could hardly believe his eyes. It was Tuesday, 13 July 1948, and instead of being home well before the 4pm from Perth came blasting up the 1 in 70 at about 30mph with two engines at its head, here it was before he got there, well early and going at nearer 40mph with a big engine on the front and the second unusually at the rear. And what an engine – a smooth, streamlined box, like nothing he had ever seen before, painted green with horizontal yellow stripes. From it came a noise unlike anything he was used to; quick rasping beats in a slightly jazzy pattern. And the first coach was an elderly oddity with a sort of bay window on the side.

What our ghillie was seeing was the most northerly of the great Interchange Trials of 1948, and the engine, No 34004 *Yeovil* of Bulleid's *West Country* class, had come from south of the Thames to knock spots off traditional Highland line train running. If he had no idea of what was happening, there were many thousands of railway enthusiasts who did, for the Railway Executive had announced details of the programme (see table 1) back in March; they were to last from mid-April to early September, ranging from Inverness to London, Leeds to Plymouth. Fourteen different types of locomotives were to take part; many would find themselves in areas of the country they had never visited before, and were unlikely to see again. Their drivers, too, would

Bulleid Pacific No 35017 Belgian Marine *with LMS tender attached for water pick up purposes awaits departure from Nine Elms shed before crossing London for one of the Interchange trials. The probable dates (both Mondays) are 10 May 1948 light engine to Camden or 24 May 1948, en route to Kings Cross.*

LNER class A4 Pacific No E22 Mallard (the original and provisional BR renumbering) and an unknown SR Lord Nelson class 4-6-0 stand side by side on Nine Elms shed, June 1948.

Mallard *alongside the coal crane at Nine Elms shed. There appears to be a form of spring balance above the bucket so it is reasonable to assume that the coal is being weighed in readiness for the 'trial' on 8 June 1948.*

often be involved in a Cook's tour of unfamiliar Britain. Technicians recording their performances would be busy, week after week, trundling round the country; the Doncaster based team, for instance, went to London, Leeds, Manchester, Inverness and South Wales.

So, a never to be repeated Pandora's Box of unexpected good things for the enthusiast; a great deal of detailed planning to get everything and everybody in the right places at the right times. What was it all in aid of?

Robert Riddles, the Member of the Railway Executive for Mechanical Engineering, was an LMS man born and bred, and had seen that company's range of modern locomotives, from three chief mechanical engineers, become national leaders in terms of overall capability, efficiency and maintenance, and adapted to meet the challenge of postwar conditions. Of the locomotives of the other three railways, many of the former GWR classes were considered obsolescent. The non-electrified areas of the Southern were operated by the prima donna Bulleid Pacifics backed up by small numbers of modern engines and an array of museum pieces. And on the LNER Gresley's three cylinder engines, while often showing brilliance of performance, were expensive to build and both they and the later Thompson machines needed more maintenance than the equivalent LMS breed. It was an unhappy forecast for the years ahead.

Riddles' principal officers at the Railway Executive were all ex LMS men. It would have been perfectly natural, to continue building LMS types for all line use; indeed, to a degree this was done as a stop-gap measure during the first four transitional years. But the politics of such a move – and they *had* to be considered – could only be fraught. So it was very much a part of Riddles' ethos, that a new and comprehensive range of locomotive designs should be produced, incorporating the best modern features within the philosophy of simplicity, to meet the foreseeable conditions of operation in the 1950s and beyond. Hence the Interchange Trials of 1948.

The programme of exchanges was co-ordinated by the chief operating manager of the London Midland Region. It involved three groups of locomotives; large express passenger, mixed traffic and heavy freight, and in each case drivers from the parent Region handled the engine for both *home* and *away* tests. This led to problems with inadequate route knowledge on *foreign* lines; each driver had just two round trips on Monday to Thursday to learn such routes before the test runs, under the guidance of a *home* conductor. This brief familiarisation did not give the driver more than a rough impression and left him heavily dependent on his conductor, who was usually on a strange engine. The actual test runs comprised two round trips on Tuesday to Friday of the following week with the dynamometer car, to produce full data on coal and water consumptions, work done and other items. Drivers were given no uniform briefing on whether fuel economy was paramount or whether to demonstrate what their engines were capable of. The result was some extreme variation in performance.

Five express passenger types were tested. The three Pacifics – the ex LNER A4, the ex LMS Duchess and the ex SR Merchant Navy were all classed 7P at the time (this subsequently became 8P) as was the ex GWR 4-6-0 King. The odd man out, the ex LMS rebuilt Royal Scot was one power class lower and usually took slightly lower loads. These

*One of the LMS 'big locomotives'
used in the 1948 exchange trials was
No 46236 City of Bradford. The
Bishop did not manage to
photograph it on any of the
exchange runs but this early BR shot
(full British Railways lettering) with
a Euston–Holyhead train of ex LMS
stock passing under Hampstead
Road bridge, (note the trolley bus)
catches the scene much as it would
have been at the time.*

*The SR Merchant Navy class used
for the 'foreign' trials was No 35017
Belgian Marine and the London
Midland Region train chosen the
10.00 am Euston–Glasgow Royal
Scot between Euston and Carlisle.
Belgian Marine, complete with SR
headcode discs, is seen here climbing
Shap on Wednesday 5 May 1948.*

engines worked the Kings Cross–Leeds Central, Euston–Carlisle, Paddington–Plymouth and Waterloo–Exeter Central routes.

All the mixed traffic engines were two cylinder 4-6-0s in class 5 except one, the ex SR West Country Pacific, which had much greater power potential and power classification 6. The other contenders were the ex GWR Hall, the Stanier class 5 from the LMS and the ex LNER Thompson B1. They covered the rather more difficult routes: St Pancras–Manchester Central, Marylebone–Manchester London Road, Bristol–Plymouth, and Perth–Inverness. The freight engines used, all in power class 8F were the ex LMS Stanier 8F, the ex LNER 01, the ex GWR 28XX and the Riddles ex War Department engine, all 2-8-0s. In addition the Riddles WD 2-10-0 was tested. The Southern had no comparable machine to offer. These tests on unfitted mineral trains up to 1100 tons weight covered Acton–Severn Tunnel Junction, New England (Peterborough)–Hornsey, Toton (Nottingham)–Brent, and a cross country route between Bristol and Eastleigh. Because of gauge problems the ex-GWR engines were barred from London Midland routes, and, moreover, the King was not allowed on the Waterloo–Exeter run, and the Hall could not work Perth–Inverness.

Three dynamometer cars were available to record performance; they were the ex LMS No 1 car and those of the GWR and LNER, and as far as possible they ran behind each locomotive over the car's own ground: the Swindon car recorded the Waterloo–Exeter tests of all the contenders throughout the month of June.

Treacy first heard of the Trials from a radio announcement, and through his railway and enthusiast contacts soon put together details of the workings – only to find that his official engagements as Rector of Keighley, and the severe petrol rationing then in force, precluded him from photographing many of the very attractive possibilities on offer. In May he spent two days on Shap, catching up first with No 35017 *Belgian Marine* on the down Royal Scot, and two weeks later with No 60034 *Lord Faringdon*. In subsequent weeks he went to Beeston Junction, three miles out of Leeds, to get pictures of the 07.50 up train with No 6018 *King Henry VI* working hard to make speed for the stiff rise to Ardsley, and *Belgian Marine* again. Finally, in early

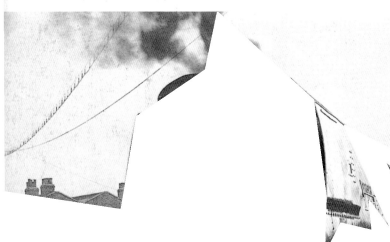

*The mixed traffic engine chosen by
the Southern for the St Pancras–
Manchester trial was No 34005
Barnstaple and as such it was
booked to leave Nine Elms at 05.30
on Monday 21 June. It must be
assumed that Barnstaple was
photographed by Eric Treacy whilst
preparing for a regular Nine Elms
duty but had (as with Belgian
Marine) been coupled to a standard
LMS tender.*

June, Waterloo and Nine Elms shed saw him recording two of his favourite classes, the A4 *Mallard* and Royal Scot No 46154 *The Hussar*, the latter with its temporary eight wheeled WD tender.

Among the general public and railway enthusiasts, the Trials raised keen and partisan interest. Naturally, professional railwaymen also wanted to know all about their 'foreign' competitors. On sheds and at stations, drivers, firemen, inspectors, managers and fitters could be seen studying them, looking for the features which differed from those they knew. Cab layouts were studied, exhaust beats listened to with practised ear, visiting drivers quizzed in the messroom on the finer points of their mounts. Tremendous regional loyalties were stimulated. It manifested itself in little ways; the WD tenders coupled to the Duchess and Royal Scot on the Southern's waterless wastes was mysteriously lettered LMS, a one-off inscription to which they were never entitled!

At this time World War II had been over for barely three years and its ravages were still much in evidence. Passenger train timings were generally far from pre-war standards, 240 minutes running time from Leeds to Kings Cross (186.3 miles) with five stops, and a dismal 103 minutes non stop for the 83.8 miles from Waterloo to Salisbury were typical. Yet other routes called for really hard running to keep time, none more so than the Great Central line to Manchester. While most routes were happily free from permanent way restrictions, after the deferred maintenance of the war years, some were in quite deplorable condition. The West Coast main line averaged eleven such temporary restrictions – on occasion up to fourteen! – and the Midland route to Manchester was not much better. Some routes also suffered a plethora of signal delays. Together these factors went far to invalidate certain of the test results.

In the express passenger category, only one engine went through its whole test series, the ex LMS Duchess No 46236, *City of Bradford*. The Royal Scot No 46162 *Queen's Westminster Rifleman* would have done so but was damaged in a collision while at Crewe to have the WD tender fitted for tests on the Southern. The A4s let themselves down badly with two hot inside big ends which caused test cancellations. The Southern seemed to experience some difficulty in finding a suitable Merchant Navy or West Country, using three of each. Only the use of locally-based mixed traffic engines prevented class 5 No 45253 and B1 No 61251 also running the whole series.

Punctuality in some cases left much to be desired, thanks to delays and uninspiring driving. The Kings Cross–Leeds route was generally good in this respect, the West Coast often lamentable. Undoubtedly the two engines whose performance sparkled were the Royal Scot and the West Country. Driver Brooker from Camden on the two Scots produced some particularly fine running on the Leeds route with gross loads well over 500 tons, on the Exeter–Waterloo tests with almost equal loads, and at times on the Western Region. The three West Countries also gave some splendid demonstrations of their sheer power; Driver Swain from Nine Elms was the outstanding exponent, approaching the task on both the Great Central and Highland lines with great panache and a cavalier disregard for the timetable. Time and again he and his mate, Hooker, pushed their machine to turn out equivalent drawbar horsepowers nearing – and in one case exceeding

An A4 on Shap. A preliminary run with class A4 Pacific No 60034 Lord Faringdon at the head of the 10.00 am Royal Scot, Euston to Glasgow on either 17 or 19 May 1948. This photograph was probably obtained by travelling by stopping train and bicycle (or on foot) from Tebay as petrol was severely rationed at the time.

Clearance problems restricted the Great Western locomotives to their home territory or the Eastern Region with no comparative runs over either the West Coast main line or out of Waterloo. No 6018 King Henry VI passes Beeston Junction with the 07.50 Leeds Central–Kings Cross express on Friday 21 May 1948. The train is pure LNER with the ex North Eastern Railway dynamometer car as the leading vehicle.

37

Two of the larger Bulleid Pacifics were used on the Eastern Region main line, No 35019 French Line CGT on the preliminary runs and No 35017 Belgian Marine on the actual trials. Eric Treacy caught French Line CGT passing Beeston Junction, Leeds on the 07.40 Leeds Central–Kings Cross duty on 18 May 1948. Note the ex GNR somersault signals and the steam sanding apparatus at work; the Bulleid Pacifics had a propensity to slip and there was a gradient of 1 in 100.

– 2000, a figure seldom approached even by the express passenger engines.

The outcome in terms of specific coal consumption related to power produced was not unexpected. The A4 and Duchess vied closely with each other, the A4 usually having a thin edge because of higher superheat. The Royal Scot came next, while the King (with small superheater) and the Merchant Navy with its erratic cylinder performance due to the Bulleid chain driven valve gear were the least efficient. Among the mixed traffic engines, there was little to choose between the B1 and Stanier class 5; the Hall was little more efficient than the West Country (though there were some mitigating circumstances), both being markedly worse than the other two. In the freight tests, the ex GWR 28XX, the O1 and the Stanier 8F were very evenly matched. Surprisingly, perhaps, the two Riddles freight engines were slightly less efficient than the other three, despite their LMS class 8F ancestry.

The Western Region, maintaining their intense GWR pride and their odd man out status, felt the need to redeem themselves for their indifferent showing. To do so it was necessary to move the goalposts. It was argued that the use of Yorkshire and Nottinghamshire hard coal put their engines at a disadvantage as compared with the Welsh coal which the firemen were used to. A supplementary set of trials was therefore made on the three Western Region routes, using top grade Welsh coal. To add spice, additional tests between Paddington and Plymouth were run with one of the first Kings with larger superheater. It caused no surprise when the results were much more favourable, bringing the coal consumption of the standard King marginally below that of the Royal Scot and the high superheat engine nearly to that of the A4 and Duchess; there were dramatic improvements to the figures for the Hall and 28XX too. Swindon pride had been assuaged.

The comprehensive report on the Interchange Trials was issued early in 1949 and its conclusions contained little that was not already well established. But lest it should be thought that outline design work on new locomotives awaited its distilled wisdom, the Railway Executive had been busy preparing proposals for twelve types of standard locomotives while the Trials were actually in progress, and these saw the light of day in a June 1948 report. Four were, in essence, existing LMS designs (none of which figured in the Trials programme), two more were adaptations of those designs, one was a Duchess with modifications and four were completely new. In the event the modified Duchess was not needed and only one of the last four survived the reappraisal process more or less as proposed, to become the BR Standard Britannia 4-6-2.

So ended the great Interchange Trials of 1948. For the enthusiast – and Treacy was certainly that – they were splendid while they lasted. Two notable express passenger engines arrived on the scene too late to participate; the Peppercorn A1 Pacific could have been expected to show up well against the Duchess and the *rebuilt* Merchant Navy would have fought on more equal terms than in its original form. Then the last two Stanier class 5s, built under Ivatt's direction with Caprotti poppet valve gear, might well have improved still further on the achievements of their piston valve sisters.

An actual test run with SR Merchant Navy No 35017 Belgian Marine just short of Beeston Junction. As before the train is the 07.50 Leeds Central–Kings Cross and the date is Friday 28 May 1948. The home railway's dynamometer car was used for all trials except the Southern who did not possess one and borrowed the Great Western's vehicle.

It was only natural that LNER men should choose their standard bearer for at least one of the 'trials' though No E22 Mallard managed only one run over the Waterloo–Exeter main line before failing. The engine is seen here leaving at the head of the 10.50 am West of England express on Tuesday 8 June 1948. The leading coach is the GWR dynamometer car.

Somewhat understandably Eric Treacy was never able to find the time to cover the performance of the West Country Pacifics north of Perth, but he was able to obtain this photograph of No 34004 Yeovil returning home. It was caught at Shap summit piloting an unrebuilt Royal Scot on the 08.55 am Perth–Euston express as far as Crewe on Saturday 17 July 1948.

Two photographs showing LMS class 6P 4-6-0 No 46154 The Hussar on one of the preliminary runs of the 10.50 am ex Waterloo on either Monday 7 June or Wednesday 9 June 1948. As there were no water troughs on the Southern and the LMS standard tenders only held 4000 gallons it was vital to find one with a greater capacity. This was achieved by borrowing a 5000 gallon tender from a WD 2-8-0. Dynamometer cars were not attached to the preliminary runs.

Black 5 4-6-0 No 44973 represented the LMS on the trials over its home territory the Perth–Inverness Highland main line. It is seen here in the mid 1950s leaving Carlisle with a down express. During the exchanges the driver of No 44973 knowing the road made no attempt to match the pyrotechnics of West Country No 34004 or even the B1 No 61292 on the Highland gradients.

LNER B1 4-6-0 No 61251 Oliver Bury worked two trials, the WR Bristol–Plymouth and the LMR St Pancras–Manchester. Overall the B1s proved themselves the equal of the Black 5s under the test conditions. No 61251 passes Copenhagen Junction signal box with a down express in the mid 1950s.

Although not part of the Locomotive Exchanges a few years later (between 1951 and 1953) three LNER design class A1 Pacifics were sent specially to Glasgow's Polmadie shed for working over the West Coast main line route between there and Crewe. The regular return trip was at the head of the 11.25 am Birmingham New Street–Glasgow and Eric Treacy caught No 60161 North British on this turn in 1952.

INTERCHANGE TRIALS 1948 : WEEKLY PROGRAMME

Details in italics are of familiarisation runs on Monday to Thursday.
Other details are of test runs on Tuesday to Friday with dynamometer car

Week Comm.	ex LMS No 1 Car — Trains	ex LMS No 1 Car — Loco	ex LNER Car — Trains	ex LNER Car — Loco	ex GWR Car — Trains	ex GWR Car — Loco
19 April	10.00 Euston–Carlisle (Note 1) 12.55 Carlisle–Euston	Duchess 46236	13.10 Kings Cross–Leeds 07.50 Leeds–Kings Cross – do –	A4 60034 R. Scot 46162	13.30 Paddington–Plymouth 08.30 Plymouth–Paddington – do –	King 6018 M. Navy 35019
26 April		—	13.10 Kings Cross–Leeds 07.50 Leeds–Kings Cross – do –	R. Scot 46162 Duchess 46236	13.30 Paddington–Plymouth 08.30 Plymouth–Paddington – do –	M. Navy 35019 E22 (Note 7) A4 60033
3 May	10.00 Euston–Carlisle 12.55 Carlisle–Euston – do –	R. Scot 46162 M. Navy 35017	13.10 Kings Cross–Leeds 07.50 Leeds–Kings Cross	Duchess 46236	13.30 Paddington–Plymouth 08.30 Plymouth–Paddington	A4 60033
10 May	10.00 Euston–Carlisle 12.55 Carlisle–Euston	M. Navy 35017	*13.10 Kings Cross–Leeds 07.50 Leeds–Kings Cross*	*King 6018*	*13.30 Paddington–Plymouth 08.30 Plymouth–Paddington*	*Duchess 46236*
17 May	*10.00 Euston–Carlisle 12.55 Carlisle–Euston*	*A4 60034*	13.10 Kings Cross–Leeds 07.50 Leeds–Kings Cross	King 6018 M. Navy 35019	13.30 Paddington–Plymouth 08.30 Plymouth–Paddington	Duchess 46236
24 May	10.00 Euston–Carlisle 12.55 Carlisle–Euston	A4 60034	13.10 Kings Cross–Leeds 07.50 Leeds–Kings Cross – do –	M. Navy 35017	13.30 Paddington–Plymouth 08.30 Plymouth–Paddington – do –	R. Scot 46162
31 May	10.15 St Pancras–Manchester 13.50 Manchester–St Pancras	Cl.5 45253	10.00 Marylebone–Manchester 08.25 Manchester–Marylebone – do –	B1 61163 W. Country 34006	10.50 Waterloo–Exeter 12.37 Exeter–Waterloo – do –	M. Navy 35018 A4 60033 and 22 (Note 2)
7 June	*10.15 St Pancras–Manchester 13.50 Manchester–St Pancras*	*B1 61251*	10.00 Marylebone–Manchester 08.25 Manchester–Marylebone – do –	W. Country 34006	10.50 Waterloo–Exeter 12.37 Exeter–Waterloo (Note 3) – do –	A4s E22 and 60037 (note 3) R. Scot 46154
14 June	10.15 St Pancras–Manchester 13.50 Manchester–St Pancras	B1 61251 W. Country 34005	10.00 Marylebone–Manchester 08.25 Manchester–Marylebone – do –	Cl. 5 45253 Hall 6990	10.50 Waterloo–Exeter 12.37 Exeter–Waterloo – do –	R. Scot 46154 *Duchess 46236*
21 June	10.15 St Pancras–Manchester 13.50 Manchester–St Pancras – do –	W. Country 34005	10.00 Marylebone–Manchester 08.25 Manchester–Marylebone	Hall 6990	10.50 Waterloo–Exeter 12.37 Exeter–Waterloo	Duchess 46236

Date	Route	Loco	Route	Loco	Route	Loco
28 June	10.40 Brent–Toton / 09.30 Toton–Brent	8Fs 48400 and 48189 (Note 4)	—	—	13.45 Bristol–Plymouth / 13.35 Plymouth–Bristol	Hall 6990
5 July	10.40 Brent–Toton / 09.30 Toton–Brent	WD 2-8-0 63169	16.00 Perth–Inverness / 0820 Inverness–Perth	Cl.5 44973	13.45 Bristol–Plymouth / 13.35 Plymouth–Bristol	B1 61251
12 July	– do –	WD 2-10-0 73776	– do –	W. Country 34004	– do –	Cl.5 45253
19 July	10.40 Brent–Toton / 09.30 Toton–Brent	01 63789	16.00 Perth–Inverness / 0820 Inverness–Perth	B1 61292	13.45 Bristol–Plymouth / 13.35 Plymouth–Bristol	W. Country 34006
26 July	07.30 Ferme Pk–N. England / 08.05 N. England–Ferme Pk	01 63773	*11.20 Acton–Severn T Jc / 14.40 Severn T Jc–Hanwell*	8F 48189	09.45 Bristol ED–Eastleigh / 11.36 Eastleigh–Bristol ED	28xx 3803
9 Aug	07.30 Ferme Pk–N. England / 08.05 N. England–Ferme Pk	WD 2-10-0 73774	11.20 Acton–Severn T Jc / 14.40 Severn T Jc–Hanwell	28xx 3803	09.45 Bristol ED–Eastleigh / 11.36 Eastleigh–Bristol ED	WD 2-8-0 77000
16 Aug	– do –	8F 48189	– do –	WD 2-10-0 73774	– do –	01 63789
23 Aug	– do –	28xx 3803	– do –	WD 2-8-0 77000	– do –	WD 2-10-0 73774
30 Aug	07.30 Ferme Pk–N. England / 08.05 N. England–Ferme Pk	WD 2-8-0 63169	11.20 Acton–Severn T Jc / 14.40 Severn T Jc–Hanwell	01 63773	09.45 Bristol ED–Eastleigh / 11.36 Eastleigh–Bristol ED	8F 48189
22 Nov	—	—	Additional Tests using Welsh Coal	—	13.30 Paddington–Plymouth / 08.30 Plymouth–Paddington	King 6001 (Note 5)
29 Nov	—	—		—	13.45 Bristol–Plymouth / 13.35 Plymouth–Bristol	Hall 6961
6 Dec	—	—		—	11.15 Acton–Severn T Jc / 08.40 Severn T Jc–Hanwell	28xx 3864
13 Dec	—	—		—	13.30 Paddington–Plymouth / 08.30 Plymouth–Paddington (Note 6)	King 6022 (Note 5)

Notes:
1. Test on 21 April was on 1552 Carlisle–Euston due to blockage of line at Lancaster earlier in the day.
2. A4 No 60033 failed at Andover on 31 May due to hot inside big end, and replaced by No 22 for familiarisation runs on 2/3 June and test runs on 8/9 June.
3. Test on 9 June terminated at Salisbury due to failure of A4 No 22 with hot inside big end. No 60037 worked test runs on 10/11 June.
4. No 48400 was in poor mechanical condition and replaced by No 48189 for test runs on 1/2 July.
5. King No 6001 had 14-element superheater and No 6022 a 28-element superheater.
6. 17.30 Paddington–Plymouth train on 16 December.
7. E22 failed at Savernake on 27 April.

resignation in September 1949, and construction of the last ten Merchant Navy and forty West Country/Battle of Britain Pacifics kept Eastleigh and Brighton works occupied for a while. These engines showed no significant changes from earlier examples, though a number of minor modifications improved their reliability to a degree. Riddles, whose origins were LMS, was happy enough to see this construction go ahead so long as the operators backed the need for them.

What he was *not* willing to endorse was Bulleid's authority, bulldozed through the Southern Railway Board in late 1947, for thirty-one more Leader class engines on top of the original order for five. Design and development work on this revolutionary concept was still incomplete in 1948, and even when built a lengthy proving period would be essential for such a complex machine before it could be released to traffic. In the meantime the Southern could well find itself with a dire shortage of modern locomotives. After some very anguished discussion with Bulleid (E.S. Cox has described him as the 'supreme autocrat') Riddles told him, in effect, "You can have your thirty-one engines, but they will be LMS Fairburn 2-6-4 tanks. Come back when the Leader has proved itself." Bulleid took the huff, and resigned just after the first example emerged from Brighton works. Within twelve months Riddles had been proved absolutely right and that first Leader, the only one to be completed, went for scrap.

The CME headquarters at Derby carried on for a while with little change in its plans. With the completion of the last Duchess Pacific in May 1948, and the continued rebuilding of Royal Scots and Patriots, the London Midland Region short sightedly judged that they would have adequate large power for the 1950s. Even the Patriot rebuilding came to a grinding halt in 1949. There was, however, a seemingly insatiable appetite for class 5MT 4-6-0s, and over the first four years of nationalisation, another hundred were built.

It was a class which went through an almost continuous evolutionary process to overcome weaknesses and increase repair mileage. Roller bearing axleboxes were introduced, an extended trial of the Caprotti poppet valve gear was made, and a handful of class 5s appeared with double chimneys – though not for very long. One was even built with *outside* Stephenson valve gear. All were aimed at making them more effective traffic-movers and reduce maintenance needs.

Treacy soon became familiar with the Caprotti class 5s allocated to Holbeck shed, Leeds and working over the Settle & Carlisle line. Maintenance wise they proved excellent, but unfortunately a side effect of the gear was to produce an engine which lacked all the dash of the piston valve engines when starting and hill climbing, which did not endear them to drivers though they would run like hares on the level and coast very freely downhill. Considerable tinkering with the gear brought only modest improvement. But Ivatt with Riddles' backing persevered with the manufacturers, and influenced them to go for an outside (and fully accessible) drive. The last two class 5s built in 1951 were fitted with this modified gear, including further refinement of the valve events, and this time they hit the jackpot; Nos 44686/7 proved splendid engines, strong and economical. Riddles applied this later development to thirty BR standard class 5s and also installed it on the singleton Pacific *Duke of Gloucester*, which on test gave cylinder efficiencies higher than any other simple expansion engine in the world.

Eric Treacy had little chance of taking many photographs on the Western Region and when he did these were usually at Paddington. This shot taken at the stabling point at Ranelagh Bridge locomotive yard just outside the station shows one of the thirty Castle class engines built by British Railways from 1948–50, No 7014 Caerhays Castle based at Bristol Bath Road depot (82A).

In all 110 small 4-6-2s of Oliver Bulleid's design ranged over the Southern Region from Margate to Plymouth and beyond. The first of forty BR built engines (April 1948) was No 34071 601 Squadron *seen here leaving Victoria station shortly after completion. Even so BR built No 34071 is sparkling in SR malachite green livery though recognising that the new era is dawning by the words British Railways on the tender. The leading coach is what the SR called a nondescript brake (i.e. it could be used as either a first, old second or third class vehicle) whilst the next two appear to be the 1921 design SE&C continental stock with vertical matchboard sides.*

Alone among the four companies the LMS postwar had pioneered new designs of small engines for light and middle-range work incorporating modern developments to minimise servicing and increase mileage between works repairs. The class 2 2-6-0 and 2-6-2 tank were immediately welcomed by footplate and fitting staff. The class 4 2-6-0 of 1947 was received with much less enthusiasm, being an indifferent steamer despite its enormous double chimney. After thorough tests this excrescence was replaced by a conventional single chimney which cured the problem. There was one other LMS design which was ahead of anything produced by the other companies, the Fairburn class 4 2-6-4 tank, which also incorporated the same modern features.

Using his authority at the Railway Executive, Riddles now began to sell these four machines to the other Regions until his own equivalent standard engines were ready. First a pair of 2-6-4 tanks went to the Southern in 1948, for trials; by 1950 Brighton works had embarked on building forty-one for use mainly on the Central Division of the Southern. Late in 1949, class 2 2-6-0 No 46413 was loaned to the Western Region for trials against an old 0-6-0 Dean Goods. Swindon complained about its steaming, something which men who handled

The Southern Railway's contribution to BR was also represented by Oliver Bulleid's Merchant Navy class, ten of which were constructed after nationalisation. Eric Treacy did not often travel south of London on his photographic safaris but on this occasion he found No 35027 Port Line of Stewarts Lane shed at Dover between boat train duties probably around 1950.

All the Merchant Navys and a number of the small Pacifics were later rebuilt under the auspices of R.G. Jarvis making them into sturdier simple machines. Towards the end of steam (1967 on the Southern) West Country class No 34025 Whimple stands at Waterloo heading a Bournemouth express.

The last member of the Merchant Navy class to be built (4/1949) No 35030 Elder Dempster Line *waits under the coaling plant at Nine Elms shed in July 1964. No 35030 had a short life of but eighteen years, nine in original form and nine from its rebuilding date of April 1958.*

Class 8P 4-6-2 No 46257 City of Salford *was the last of Stanier's Duchess Pacifics to be ordered by the LMS and had the misfortune to miss being an LMS locomotive by four and a half months entering traffic in May 1948. This engine and No 46256 aptly named* Sir William A. Stanier FRS *different from earlier members of the class in having roller bearing axleboxes, electric lights, self cleaning smokebox and shorter cab side sheets. The engine appears here in a typical Treacy location, Low Gill down intermediate block signal, heading an up express sometime in the summer of 1958.*

them over the fierce grades of the Cockermouth, Keswick and Penrith line had not noticed! However, tests at Swindon did increase steam production markedly by draughting alterations. By 1951 Darlington works was building them for the Eastern and North Eastern Regions and in 1952 Swindon works started production of a batch for Western Region use. The Southern Region, too, took numbers of basically similar 2-6-2 tanks. The improvement of the class 4 2-6-0 led to Doncaster and Darlington building substantial batches for the Eastern and North Eastern Regions. They virtually monopolised workings on the erstwhile Midland & Great Northern Joint in its last years.

Before nationalisation Edward Thompson as chief mechanical engineer at Doncaster had initiated two main lines of development following the Gresley regime, of which he was severely critical. First he produced a new group of Pacifics of passenger and mixed traffic capability. In fact, though capable they proved very unsatisfactory mechanically and went early and unsung to the scrap yard. Secondly he laid down a range of simple two-cylinder locomotives for secondary duties; this comprised the class B1 4-6-0, the class L1 2-6-4 tank and the rebuild of the three cylinder class K4 2-6-0 as a prototype. If Thompson's Pacifics were a severe maintenance headache, his L1 2-6-4 tanks were, if anything, worse. Only the B1 and K1 could be regarded as successful.

A strange man, Edward Thompson. After the ordered progress and occasional excitement of the Gresley years, his appointment as Chief

The north end of Carlisle Citadel station showing No 46257 City of Salford *moving off in the early 1960s, it was by that time a Carlisle based engine. This shows the class from a different viewpoint revealing details not normally seen including the four Ross-pop safety valves, the cab roof and the fact that the locomotive is now fitted with AWS (the reservoir can be seen on the running plate) and 25kv electric warning flashes.*

53

Although nominally rebuilds the LMS Royal Scots with 2A taper boilers were almost new machines. The work was spread over nearly thirteen years and No 46106 Gordon Highlander *(rebuilt 1949)* was unique for the class in having large BR smoke deflectors instead of the smaller LMS type. The engine is shown here taking water at Carlisle Citadel station around 1952.

The last two of 842 LMS class 5 4-6-0s Nos 44686/7 were built at Horwich in 1951 and were a modified design with Caprotti valve gear, high running plate and double chimney. The final engine No 44687 is seen here at Shrewsbury with a local train of three LMS coaches bound for Crewe c1958. Standing at the down main platform is Britannia Pacific No 70022 *Tornado* from Cardiff Canton shed; about to come off its train, a west to north express, and hand over to a London Midland locomotive for the remainder of the journey to Manchester or Liverpool. The Western Region Britannias were transferred to the London Midland Region in September 1961.

An LMS class 4-6-0 No 44697 (built at Horwich in 1950) stands in Leeds Central station coupled to one of the BR coal weighing tenders which were used on test runs to measure coal consumption. The engine will shortly work an express to Manchester Victoria.

Twenty additional LMS type class 5 4-6-0s were built with Caprotti valve gear (Nos 44738–57) in 1948 and one of these, No 44742 (also fitted with a self cleaning smokebox) of Llandudno Junction shed (7A) is seen here leaving Llandudno station with an up express in the summer of that year.

Mechanical Engineer, and his announcement that he had a lot to do and not much time to do it (he was within five years of retirement) must have come as a shock. As a man he was a curious mixture; austere yet self-indulgent, incommunicative yet capable of charming the birds out of the trees, a fountain of ideas, many of them quite remarkable, yet intolerant of criticism or alternative suggestions. Anyone with the temerity to question his instructions got short shrift, and it has been said that if he stooped to address any of his staff by their Christian name they were headed for the dole queue. At the bottom of it all was a profound dislike, perhaps even something deeper, of certain aspects of Gresley's work. In this there was undoubtedly some right on his side. But with his strong convictions, he did not want to be confused by facts. He would walk through the works at Doncaster, apparently looking neither to right nor left, discussing repair work in progress with nobody, foreman or man in overalls.

The LMS designed class 4MT 2-6-0 came out in 1947. One of the BR built engines No 43113 (Horwich 1951) heads an up local at Gargrave station in 1959. British Railways per se was now over ten years old and the only sign of change is the locomotive, the station nameboard and flat-bottom track.

Thompson's successor, A.H. Peppercorn, had only been in office some eighteen months at nationalisation, but he already had the designs for two new Pacifics in his armoury, and a total of sixty four A1s and A2s were produced at Doncaster and Darlington. These eliminated nearly all the weaknesses and nonsenses of both the Gresley and Thompson Pacifics, and the A1s in particular set new standards in mileage run, reliability and repair costs. They maintained an average of over 100,000 miles between works classified repairs, while the five built with roller bearings on all axles even improved on this figure. Treacy saw quite a lot of them during his visits to Leeds Central station, and their initial appearance with plain double chimneys, though far from elegant, did not seem to put him off. The replacement cast chimneys with flared tops were altogether more attractive.

Of the two cylinder designs, the B1s were built in large numbers, including orders for no less than 250 from the North British Locomotive Co. If they were not of Stanier calibre in the maintenance field, they were very willing horses and economical.

Somewhat puzzling was Riddles' acquiescence in the building of more class L1 2-6-4 tanks, after the thirty which were committed by LNER orders. They quickly proved to be quite dreadful engines, full of problems for shed repair staff and quickly knocking themselves to pieces. Yet a further seventy were authorised and built in 1949/50, mainly by contractors, when the same number of Fairburn 2-6-4s would have been a godsend to the hard-pressed depots in the London area.

There were two other oddities in the building programmes during this period. First was a tremendous appetite on the part of the Western Region for 0-6-0 pannier tanks. Between 1948 and 1956 a total of 335 was built. The more modern looking 15xx series with outside cylinders and Walschaerts valve gear numbered ten only. For stability reasons they were confined to carriage shunting and tripping between Paddington and Old Oak Common, and lasted only 13–14 years. No less than 194 were heavy shunting engines of the 94xx class, all built by contractors – Robert Stephenson, Bagnall and Yorkshire Engine. Their route availability made them unsuitable for much branch line work, and their heavy shunting role was taken over by the ubiquitous 350hp diesel electric shunter. They may have been cheap to build, but their short lives (around nine–ten years) made them an expensive investment.

Metro-Cammell class 101 dmu with the 09.41 am Carlisle–Leeds service on 14 October 1988. Thirty years on the station is still open but only as a platform with the building in private ownership and rebuilt. The signalbox and signals have been removed. (J. Makepiece)

Then the North Eastern Region decided that they could not do without a further twenty class J72 0-6-0 shunting tanks in 1949/50. This was an ex-North Eastern Railway design which had not been built since 1925! One would have thought that a whip-round on other regions could have produced twenty elderly engines suitable for station pilot work.

The 1950s saw the final flowering of steam traction in Britain, with prewar speeds restored and sometimes bettered. In general the load was borne by locomotives of pre-nationalisation ancestry, working in what had been their home territory. Strangers, however, did make interesting invasions of ex-LMS territory over this period. In 1950/1 three A1s were transferred to Polmadie shed (Glasgow) for a time and worked expresses to Crewe, finding cautious approval from enginemen. In 1960 eight Gresley A3s displaced by dieselisation took up residence at Leeds Holbeck shed to work over the Settle & Carlisle line to and from Glasgow, displacing Royal Scots to second rate work and early withdrawal. Also in that year A4s based at St Rollox and Aberdeen Ferryhill sheds began a partial takeover of the principal Glasgow–Aberdeen services. In both these cases ex-LMS men took to them approvingly, for they were complete masters of the work. Gresley's Big Engine policy had been justified. Only in isolated areas did the later BR standard engines play a leading role.

It was a time of great interest, occasionally even of joy, to the enthusiastic observer; who could fail to be thrilled by the magnificent turnout during these years of Haymarket shed's A1s, paintwork gleaming and buffers and motion burnished. They stood out against a tableau of grimy, neglected and increasingly run-down engines. Even that was not to last, for the diesels took over the East Coast main line, and by 1965 the slaughter of the big engines was well nigh complete. The final fling for express engines was in the summer of 1967 when the Bulleid Pacifics bowed out on the Bournemouth services.

The final version of the LMS class 4 2-6-4T was also perpetuated by BR with examples being built at Brighton as well as at Derby. No 42051 (Derby 1951) based on Hellifield (24H) leaves Settle around 1959 with a local train made up of three LMS non corridor coaches. Probably in LMS parlance an Inter-District set or IDZ comprising a brake third, a composite and a further brake third.

The LMS built three out of 162 of these class 4MT 2-6-0s, Horwich being the mother works though in later days they were also constructed at Doncaster and Darlington. One of the Darlington engines No 43098 is seen here crossing Selby swing bridge in the mid 1950s with an up loose coupled freight train.

Sprinter set No 150256 enters Selby on 21 September 1988 with the 13.41 Hull to Chester and Bangor service. After almost thirty years the scene has changed but not dramatically; the control cabin on the bridge has been raised. Selby North signalbox has gone as have the semaphore signals and the two middle roads through the station have been lifted as a result of the diversion of the East Coast main line in 1983. (J. Makepeace)

59

One of the Brighton built (LMS design) 2-6-4 tanks – note the extra SR lamp brackets – leaves Leeds City (formerly Wellington) with an express for Bradford around 1958. The first six coaches are Great Western so this may well be The Devonian from Paignton.

Two generations of banking engines stand outside Beattock shed (68D) awaiting their next turn of duty in the mid 1950s. On the left is Caledonian 0-4-4T No 55237 of class 431 (LMS 2P) built at St Rollox in 1922 especially for banking duties. On the right Fairburn 2-6-4T No 42192 built by BR in 1948. Everything has now been swept away by electrification with the shed closing in 1967 and the station following in January 1972.

Keswick station looking west in the early 1950s with a Penrith bound train leaving behind LMS designed class 2 2-6-0 No 46455 which was built at Crewe in 1950 and appears to be almost new. These engines were drafted in to Penrith and Workington sheds to replace the ageing LNWR Webb 18-inch goods 0-6-0s which until then monopolised all services.

The LMS light 2-6-0 and 2-6-2 tanks incorporating modern developments to minimise servicing and repair costs came out in 1946 and were heartily welcomed by locomotive crews. Class 2 2-6-2T No 41265 of Manningham shed (Bradford) leaves Leeds City Midland side with a local for Bradford, Ilkley or Skipton in the early 1950s.

The class B1 4-6-0 was the LNER's reply to the LMS class 5. A total of 410 was built with 274 emerging in LNER days the remainder by BR. The majority of B1s were built by the North British Locomotive Company, fifty by the Vulcan Foundry, sixty at Darlington and ten at Gorton. In this photograph Eric Treacy achieved a handsome locomotive portrait of No E1288 built by NBL in February 1948 and seen at York in the spring of the same year.

Another pure LNER class which did not appear until after nationalisation was the K1 2-6-0 – the design was based on the Thompson two cylinder rebuild of the Gresley three cylinder K4 No 3445 renumbered 1997 in 1946. There were seventy engines in the class all built by the North British Locomotive Company in 1949 and 1950. No 62005, the preserved example of the class, is seen here on the 70ft turntable at York North mpd about 1964.

The highly polished front ends of LBSCR 0-4-2 Gladstone, the LNER's Green Arrow and Mallard plus NER 2-2-4T Aerolite around A turntable of the National Railway Museum. The clean and tidy site is in marked comparison with the typical post war steam shed.

K1 class No 62009 (new in July 1949) heads an up goods carrying through freight headlamps out of York station probably in August 1949. On the left of the photograph can be seen the goods lines from Severus Junction avoiding the station and the roundhouses of York South shed. The signals are a mixture of NER lower quadrants and LNER upper quadrants soon to be replaced by colour lights.

The summer of 1950 saw Peppercorn Pacific class A1 No 60136 (later named Alcazar) leaving Kings Cross with the down White Rose whilst to the right of the picture, alongside platform 8, is a set of LNER post war pressure ventilated steel panelled stock built for the Flying Scotsman service.

Opposite: Leeds Central station in 1952 with Peppercorn class A1 Pacific No 60123 H A Ivatt leaving with an up express. The locomotive is in the short lived BR blue livery and is allocated to Ardsley. No 60123 is electric light equipped – something which only lasted for a brief period.

Peppercorn class A2 Pacific No 60538 Velocity still with its ugly unlipped chimney stands at the up side of the island platform at Berwick upon Tweed around 1952. A total of fifteen engines was built, fourteen after nationalisation; No 60538 was outshopped at Doncaster in June 1948.

Big Four Grouping Locomotives built after Nationalisation

A total of 1,538 regional locomotives was built by British Railways between 1948 and 1956. These comprised the following classes.

Portrait of an A2. Eric Treacy was busy in the York area in the summer of 1948 and caught No 60535 Hornets Beauty (built Doncaster May 1948) resplendent in LNER green. Note the BTH type speed indicator on the left hand side trailing coupled crankpin.

BRIGHTON	34	SR West Country class	4-6-2
	41	LMS class 4	2-6-4T
CREWE	1	LMS Coronation class	4-6-2
	50	LMS class 5	4-6-0
	45	LMS class 2	2-6-0
	110	LMS class 2	2-6-2T
DARLINGTON	23	LNE class A1	4-6-2
	20	LNE class B1	4-6-0
	29	LNE class L1	2-6-4T
	28	NER class J72	0-6-0T
	37	LMS class 4	2-6-0
	38	LMS class 2	2-6-0
DERBY	106	LMS class 4	2-6-4T
	10	LMS class 2	2-6-2T
DONCASTER	26	LNE class A1	4-6-2
	14	LNE class A2	4-6-2
	50	LMS class 4	2-6-0
EASTLEIGH	10	SR Merchant Navy class	4-6-2
	6	SR West Country class	4-6-2
GORTON	10	LNE class B1	4-6-0
HORWICH	50	LMS class 5	4-6-0
	72	LMS class 4	2-6-0
	5	LMS class 0	0-4-0ST
SWINDON	30	GWR Castle class	4-6-0
	49	GWR Modified Hall class	4-6-0
	10	GWR Manor class	4-6-0
	2	GWR 2251 class	0-6-0
	20	GWR 51XX class	2-6-2T
	10	GWR 15XX class	0-6-0PT
	70	GWR 16XX class	0-6-0PT
	21	GWR 57XX class	0-6-0PT
	20	GWR 67XX class	0-6-0PT
	20	GWR 74XX class	0-6-0PT
	25	LMS class 2	2-6-0
NORTH BRITISH LOCO CO	106	LNE class B1	4-6-0
	70	LNE class K1	2-6-0
	35	LNE class L1	2-6-4T
ROBERT STEPHENSON & HAWTHORNS	35	LNE class L1	2-6-4T
	100	GWR 94XX class	0-6-0PT
W.G. BAGNALL	50	GWR 94XX class	0-6-0PT
YORKSHIRE ENGINE CO	50	GWR 94XX class	0-6-0PT

The original Fort William station taken from one of the Loch Linnhe steamer piers. This view shows a K1 2-6-0 with a four coach Mallaig service in April 1959. The track through the nearest platform (No 1) extended beyond the station buildings to the fish loading bays further down the loch shore. In June 1975 a new station was built further up the line towards Mallaig Junction.

BRITISH RAIL'S
STANDARD LOCOMOTIVES

With a great deal of hissing air from open cylinder cocks the engine was drawn slowly out of the erecting shop doors by the works shunter. It was still in its matt dusky-pink primer, although wheels and frames had acquired their first coat of black; at this stage it still lacked its tender. It proved to be a small Pacific with wide Belpaire firebox; the overall proportions were somewhat reminiscent of the little Indian standard XA Pacifics. Closer examination showed that it had bar frames, rather than the universal plate type of modern British practice, though the springing was not equalised. The outside-framed bogie with its Timken roller bearing axleboxes attracted attention.

As the shunter set the engine back on to its waiting tender, which was very angular and looked rather like that of a WD 2-8-0 but mounted on only three axles, the eye was drawn to the cab with its one-piece floor cantilevered back to the tender bulkhead. Both injectors were mounted on the fireman's side, and the cab front was vee-d. A glance above the smoke deflectors showed the sizeable but shapely double chimney and the linkage for the multiple-valve regulator. When the smokebox door came into view, the number plate could be seen to carry the figures 73000.

Then our watcher awoke. It *had* been a dream, its theme the outline class 5 mixed traffic 4-6-2 in the BR standard range, which was jettisoned in favour of the cheaper 4-6-0.

The whole idea of standardised steam locomotives for service on the railways of Britain had a shaky passage over the years, thanks to the practice of each railway designing – and usually building – its own engines. Outside contractors might get some degree of standardisation in the export field, mainly of boilers, cylinders and motion, and wheels and axles, but this seldom cut any ice with home railways. In the 1920s, Beyer Peacock offered the LMS the benefit of their design experience for an initial order for three Garratts, only to be told firmly to do it the Midland way. The results were grim! Only in the aftermath of two world wars, during each of which large numbers of a single type had been produced for War Department use were a lot of surplus locomotives snapped up cheaply by other railways.

After World War I the Great Central Robinson 2-8-0 type was sold not only to the Great Central/LNER but also to the GWR and the LNWR/LMS. The seventy five engines taken over by the LMS had short lives and were withdrawn between 1928 and 1933 though their tenders lived on, coupled to ex-LNWR Claughtons and others. A hundred were bought by the GWR and fifty were soon modified to suit Swindon practice; the remainder were quickly scrapped. In 1948 there were still forty-five at work. On their home territory the LNER began to fit other boilers with round-topped fireboxes; with Edward Thompson arriving as the chief mechanical engineer, an extensive rebuilding was set in motion amounting almost to a new engine, using the same boiler and cylinders as on the class B1 4-6-0s. This became the LNER's standard class O1 and the company's standard-bearer in the freight field in the 1948 Interchange Trials.

Riddles WD 2-8-0 No 90210 leaves the east end of the then new Healey Mills marshalling yard around 1966. The load is made up of empty 16 ton all steel mineral wagons. The running lines split here with the down roads towards Wakefield on the north side and the up lines on the south side with Healey Mills yard in between.

WD class 8F 2-8-0 No 90359, an ex Western Region locomotive as it has both types of lamp bracket, heads the Long Meg anhydrite empties between Ribblehead and Blea Moor around 1958.

69

Some 935 Austerity 2-8-0s were built for service at home and overseas during the latter part of World War II of which total 733 were eventually owned by BR, 200 by acquisition from the LNER and the remainder purchased in 1949. No 90070 (LNER No 3070) takes water at the south end of Dringhouses yard York – probably on a running in turn from Darlington works as there is little coal in the tender and the engine appears to be clean and newly painted.

Skipton around 1960. A WD class 8F 2-8-0 No 90155 comes off the Ilkley line at the head of a Haverton Hill–Heysham ICI tank train. The two empty wagons at each end are the mandatory barrier vehicles on all trains conveying petrol, oil or dangerous chemicals in steam days, a fire precaution not necessary with diesel or electric haulage.

Skipton 1988. A comparative shot still looking towards Leeds taken a generation later. Steam has been gone for twenty and more years. The station has been cleaned up but the platforms are now rationalised. Three car Pacer dmu Class 144 No 144022 shunts to work a return service to Leeds on 14 October 1988. (J. Makepeace)

Contemporary with this distribution of Robinson 2-8-0s in the early 1920s were efforts by the Association of Railway Locomotive Engineers (ARLE) to introduce new standard designs. The ARLE consisted of some thirty chief mechanical engineers and locomotive superintendents, and acted as a discussion forum. The Government asked the ARLE to prepare designs for modern locomotives which might usefully be produced in Government workshops, as a stopgap measure to ease the rundown to peacetime production. In the event the design of two-cylinder 2-8-0 and 2-6-0 locomotives took so long on a committee basis that progress was overtaken by events, and no standard engine got anywhere near production.

A Riddles 2-10-0 No 90772 from Motherwell shed leaves Beattock down goods loop to tackle the arduous ten miles ahead with a mixture of vans, opens, a tank wagon and towards the rear a large steel plate loaded on a trestle. The whole ensemble is banked by an LMS 2-6-4 tank.

1939 once more brought the need for freight and shunting engines in large numbers, with overseas use in mind, and R.A. Riddles (hitherto Mechanical & Electrical Engineer, Scotland of the LMS) was seconded to the Ministry of Supply with responsibility for procuring railway material for the forces. For very sound reasons he selected the LMS Stanier class 8F 2-8-0 for military use. The first was not delivered until France was toppling and deliveries were stopped at 208; those engines which had not been sent overseas – to Egypt, Palestine and Persia – were taken over by the LMS in 1943 – with gratitude.

Meanwhile the LNER, GWR and SR, not without strong protest, had been persuaded to build Stanier 2-8-0s in their own workshops for general use (though they were not allocated to SR depots) and between 1943 and 1946 a total of 313 was built. 'Foreign' men did not generally take them to their hearts, though they played a valuable role in Scotland. For a time during the war they were freely used on passenger work on the Aberdeen and Highland lines. On the LNER they became class O6, but all were returned to the LMS before the end of 1947. The class 8F had been a very brief standard.

In the changed conditions after Dunkirk the War Department made a new appraisal of the likely needs for military locomotives to support and follow up a planned invasion of Europe. There was a new emphasis on utter simplicity, no unnecessary frills, and the minimising of steel castings content which was a bottleneck in military supply; the end product was to be regarded as expendable. Riddles therefore organised the mass-production of an 'Austerity' 2-8-0, based on the Stanier engine, together with a 2-10-0 with restricted axle loads, North British Locomotive Co doing the design work. A total of 935 2-8-0s and 150 2-10-0s was built by that firm and Vulcan Foundry before production ceased in September 1945. Until shipment abroad began in October 1944, over 550 were working in Britain. Eventually over 900 2-8-0s and over 100 2-10-0s were shipped across the Channel.

With the peace, large numbers of both types became surplus to War Department needs; some were purchased by overseas railways – Syria, Greece and Hong Kong took small numbers, the devastated Netherlands Railways a total of 287 of both arrangements, two of which ended up in Sweden. But the great majority, no longer thought of as

One of Eric Treacy's comparatively rare photographs of a Western Region scene shows Britannia No 70025 Western Star leaving Paddington c1955, one of fifteen members of the class allocated to ex Great Western territory. Western Star is allocated to Cardiff Canton (86C), where the WR Britannias were concentrated from 1957 displacing the GWR Castles. This would be a South Wales train although it is not possible to confirm the departure time as the WR did not publish the reporting numbers in the service timetable.

73

expendable, were offered to the railways of Britain, where with high levels of traffic and postwar scrapping of worn-out engines, they were accepted, though with varying degrees of enthusiasm. The LNER had the greatest need, and the GWR and SR took batches in order to release Stanier 2-8-0s for return to the LMS. Ultimately 733 2-8-0s and twenty five 2-10-0s were purchased, 200 by the LNER and the remainder by BR after being on loan. The 2-8-0s became another semi-standard class; when spare boilers, slightly modified, were built in the 1950s, they were classed BR11 in the standard range.

The WDs had some very good features; they were powerful and gutsy, they steamed well, the injectors were very reliable, and preparation was simple. They also had some bad aspects; in particular the tenders were prone to derailment, and the absence of reciprocating balance made footplate conditions very rough when coasting. A programme of modifications was quickly undertaken to bring them up to acceptable mechanical standards and to improve the cabs to overcome objections from the footplate staff.

They were not beautiful, and their almost perpetual state of grime did nothing to enhance their appearance but they proved very capable. Who could fail to be impressed by the sight and sound of a pair of them working hard on the iron ore trains from Glasgow General Terminus to Ravenscraig, which weighed well over 1000 tons and ran on special accelerated timings. And they were not above tackling passenger work, particularly at Lancashire Wakes weeks, though it was an unpleasant experience for the enginemen and not too comfortable for the passengers in the first couple of coaches either!

Riddles had by now been appointed the member of the Railway Executive responsible for mechanical engineering, and 'one-offs' in the freight field was not what he had in mind for the unified British Railways. He saw the need for a comprehensive fleet of standard locomotives, from the largest to the smallest, passenger, mixed traffic and freight, progressively to take over the work of existing company designs. These had rarely been adapted in any way to the evolving needs of the postwar years; they were mostly labour-intensive in servicing, out of tune with the full employment era which was dawning. This was particularly so with the smaller engines, usually elderly and down graded from more important work; reliability, mechanical performance and mileage between works repairs had gone out of the window with their reduced status. Then there were the enginemen to consider; very rudimentary cabs gave them little shelter and often not even a seat to sit on.

So Riddles specified that his new standard range of locomotives should be simple but rugged, with no more than two outside cylinders unless power requirements made another essential. They would have generous bearing surfaces and would be easy to prepare, if necessary without a pit. They would have rocking grates, hopper ashpans, and self-cleaning smokeboxes which need not be opened for a week or a fortnight at a time, speeding up servicing. They would have plenty of adhesion, they would be thermally efficient (within the limitations of any simple non-condensing locomotive) and their cabs would be comfortable workplaces with good weather protection. From the workshop point of view they would provide for maximum standardisation of repairable and renewable fittings. Having satisfied all these

Baby sisters of the more successful Britannias the Clans were not popular engines. Only ten were ever built being allocated to Polmadie shed Glasgow. No 72003 is seen here climbing Beattock bank near one of Eric Treacy's favourite spots Harthope intermediate block signal. The train is a Carlisle–Glasgow local with parcels vans added to its coaches.

A most interesting photograph showing Clan class 4-6-2 No 72008 Clan Macleod approaching Beattock Summit with an unusual train. The first and last vans are LMS fifty foot full brakes, behind the leading vehicle is the Southern's cinema coach and generator van (probably painted green) whilst the fourth is an L&Y inspection saloon based at Inverness – it may well be en route there in this picture.

criteria, they would also have a uniform style to make them readily recognisable.

Certain envisaged locomotives for the range fell at early fences. For the heaviest express passenger work a multi-cylindered Pacific would be needed, and early diagrams showed basically a four-cylinder LMS Duchess but with bar frames, eight-wheeled WD-type tender and other changes. But there had been extensive recent building of big Pacifics at Doncaster, Darlington and Eastleigh, and there was no need of more. In the event a single locomotive in this category was built, but it was very different from the projected engine.

At the next stage down, a pair of class 7 two-cylinder Pacifics was proposed, identical except for having 6ft 6in and 6ft coupled wheels. It hardly needed the 1948 Interchange Trials to show that such a small step in wheel diameter was not justified; the LMS class 5s with 6ft wheels for instance were no strangers to 90mph. In the event the design crystallised around 6ft 2in wheels, the LNER and recent SR standard, and emerged as the 4-6-2 Britannia.

Another casualty was the idea of a class 5 Pacific. It was very much a border-line case. Compared with 4-6-0s such as the Thompson B1 and the Stanier class 5 it was heavier and more costly to build, and would only have come into its own on the hardest (and relatively sparse) class 5 jobs. In the end the 4-6-0 with Stanier class 5 tapered boiler won the day.

Then there was to be a heavy mixed traffic 2-8-2 with 5ft 3in coupled wheels, in a way an updating of the Gresley class P1 idea and fitted

Class 8P 4-6-2 No 71000 Duke of Gloucester was the only three cylinder BR standard locomotive; it was a nominal replacement for the ill fated No 46202 Princess Anne. No 71000 spent all of its short life at Crewe North shed and is seen here hauling the up Midday Scot at Bessie Ghyll south of Penrith around 1955. This unique locomotive has been restored from a virtual scrap condition to full working order.

BRITISH RAIL'S STANDARD LOCOMOTIVES

with the Britannia boiler. It would have been an extremely versatile machine, but Riddles demurred because adhesion would have been no greater than on existing 2-8-0s, while the brake power for working unfitted freight trains could only be increased at the cost of some complication. With an over-the-shoulder glance to his WD 2-10-0s he plumped for a big 2-10-0 instead; within the BR loading gauge the coupled wheels under the firebox could be no larger than 5ft diameter and the boiler had to be a little smaller. It looked a pure freight engine, but in service its capabilities were to surprise many people.

Between January 1951, when the first Britannia 4-6-2 no 70000 was completed at Crewe works, and March 1960 when the last 2-10-0 No 92220 *Evening Star* emerged from Swindon, a total of 999 BR standard steam locomotives was produced in seven different main works. Surprisingly in view of what had happened postwar on the LNER and GWR none was built by private contractors. The total builds of each class varied from the single big express passenger engine no 71000 *Duke of Gloucester* (actually authorised as a replacement for the ill-fated rebuild of the LMS Turbomotive of 1935, no 46202 *Princess Anne*) to 251 of the class 9F 2-10-0s, 172 class 5 4-6-0s and 155 class 4 2-6-4 tanks. They roamed the country from Ramsgate to Fort William and from Wales to East Anglia. The Western Region was most reluctant to accept BR standard engines other than 2-10-0s, while the London Midland Region was prepared to take them in large numbers, except for the Swindon-designed class 3 tender and tank engines! The impact that the BR standard locomotives made in service varied considerably, both according to type and the region on which they were running.

No 71000 Duke of Gloucester takes a down express past Kingmoor locomotive depot Carlisle probably in 1958. The train carries roof boards and may be the Birmingham–Scotland service, either the Glasgow or the Edinburgh portion running as separate trains.

An uncommon class for the Settle–Carlisle line BR standard class 5 4-6-0 No 73045 of Leeds Holbeck shed (20A) approaches Ais Gill with an eleven coach up relief (M602) train around 1955.

Edinburgh Princes Street, the one time Caledonian and LMS terminus around 1956 with standard class 5 4-6-0 No 73056 leaving with a local for Carstairs the junction with the Glasgow main line. Note the continuance of Caledonian practice with the route indicator on the centre buffer beam. Two interesting coaches are visible, a lavatory brake third and a lavatory 1st/3rd composite. The site is now a car park and part of the concourse has been incorporated into the Caledonian Hotel as a bar.

The lone class 8P no 71000 *Duke of Gloucester* spent its short life at Crewe North shed. It has been described by E.S. Cox as a 'near miss' but perhaps it might more aptly have been likened to the curate's egg. The performance and efficiency of its cylinders were quite outstanding as a result of the Caprotti poppet valve gear, but they were badly let down by the boiler, which despite its larger grate and double blastpipe was unable to match the steam output of the Britannia. At higher outputs the coal consumption soared but to no avail. The Crewe men who handled it on the overnight Perth sleeper, a 292 mile lodging turn, developed a healthy dislike for it considering that it had been sponsored by the Coal Board. It was soon kept off this job and confined to workings to and from Euston. It was withdrawn, unloved and unmourned, late in 1962 after a mileage of less than 300,000.

The Britannias, by contrast, were a successful design. If the Western Region men were not impressed those on the Eastern Region were quick to show just what they were capable of. From July 1951, a new interval service between Liverpool Street and Norwich in 2hr 10min was designed around them, and the Britannias were expected to keep this schedule, with a little in reserve, on 9-coach trains of 300 tons tare. The formidable L.P. Parker, the Great Eastern section's motive power chief, galvanised his district officers and inspectors to bring out their full potential, and the standards of footplate work and performance were impressive. Suddenly 90mph became normal at several places north of Ipswich, and little less between Chelmsford and Colchester. Most of the engines were manned by two, or sometimes three regular

Eric Treacy's original intentions included a determination only to take his photographs in sunshine but different circumstances require different approaches – the last days of steam simply had to be recorded. Hence this dull weather shot of the approaches to Chester General station (GW & LNW Joint) with standard class 5 4-6-0 No 73073 on an up empty stock train from the North Wales coast in the early 1960s. The bridge behind carries the CLC line into Northgate station. Northgate locomotive depot is to the right.

The Carlisle goods lines to the west of Citadel station are now closed and lifted except for a short section connecting the NER and LNW lines to the old Maryport and Carlisle. Sometime in 1955–7 class 5 4-6-0 No 73062 of Motherwell shed (66B) heads south passing Bog Junction (Carlisle No 10) signalbox with a train of empty double bolster wagons. The northbound train on the left is loaded with steel billets probably bound for Motherwell.

Standard Five. One of the more popular (but fewer) engines fitted with Caprotti valve gear 4-6-0 No 73152 heads south over the Forth Bridge with a local passenger train for Glasgow around 1956. The engine is based at St Rollox (65B) shed whilst the stock is a mixed bag, two Gresley LNER corridors, two BR MkI vehicles with an LNER corridor bringing up in the rear.

crews, and their outward appearance left nothing to be desired. In 1958, dieselisation of the Norwich service released Britannias for an accelerated Clacton business service. They were unique in figuring centrally in the advertising – 'fast trains every morning and evening by BRITANNIA to town'.

By contrast the London Midland men on the Western Division, with a much more *laissez faire* management outlook, did not detect any real superiority over a rebuilt Royal Scot, nor was any demanded by the nature of their work. Only on the Midland Division were they urged to some very lively running when dieselisation elsewhere made some available for that route.

The Clans, the baby sisters of the Britannias, were not a successful class. Though they showed up fairly well when an inspector was present, their steaming was not above reproach and unless driven fairly hard their running did not shine. Only ten were built; they were intended for the Highland main line but were allocated to Polmadie shed to work the Glasgow–Manchester expresses and other less arduous duties. Fifteen more were ordered in the 1952 programme for the Southern and Scottish regions, but were cancelled. The Scots already had the measure of them, and maybe the Southern managers, too, learned enough to compare their work unfavourably with the sheer elan of the Bulleid light Pacifics!

The standard class 5s were another design which produced strongly divergent views in different regions. The London Midland men, generally found them inferior to their own Stanier class 5s, complained that they were shy for steam and did not seem to do their work so willingly. Yet those which went to the Southern were actively welcomed, with Bournemouth and Stewarts Lane men holding them to be little inferior to a West Country. The elite Branksome men regarded them as every bit the equal of or even having the edge over the Stanier class 5s on the Somerset and Dorset Joint line. Praise indeed! The Scottish drivers got fair service from them on a wide variety of work and routes. The thirty engines with Caprotti valve gear were held in higher esteem than the piston valve engines, echoing experience with the last two Ivatt class 5s.

The class 4 4-6-0s and 2-6-4 tanks were, of course, confined to secondary and cross-country work, though the Shrewsbury–Aberystwyth line could be very taxing. The 4-6-0s were competent enough, but when really up against it the steaming could give rise to anxiety. A number of them were fitted with double blastpipes and chimneys to give them rather more up their sleeves, but it was not a great improvement. The 2-6-4 tanks covered a very wide range of work, from the Southern's heavy outer suburban trains on the steeply-graded Oxted route, and the sharply timed Tring and Bletchley trains out of Euston, to the farcical one-coach shuttle on the Killin branch in Scotland. They were reckoned not quite the equal of the ex-LMS breed, a little heavier on water and weaker if the boiler pressure was allowed to fall. Nevertheless, some of them working in the Glasgow area, regularly double manned, were a joy to behold in their glossy lined black livery with bright brass and copper.

The smaller class 3 and 2 engines, both tender and tank, seldom had the opportunity to draw attention to themselves, but in isolated areas they made a real impact. The BR standard class 2s in the 78xxx series,

Standard class 4 4-6-0 No 75031 attacks Camden bank on the slow (four rail electrified) line around 1957. The train is almost certainly an evening semi-fast and is formed of seven LMS non-corridor coaches.

The previous member of the class No 75030 of Bletchley shed (1E) again on the slow line passing Camden with one of the evening semi-fast trains from Euston to Tring or Bletchley around 1954. The train should be a standard seven coach Euston to Watford set seen in the previous photograph but the leading brake has been replaced with a Stanier corridor brake third in red and cream.

An unusual Treacy picture taken near one of his regular haunts, Leeds Holbeck, showing a class 3 standard 2-6-0 No 77001 on a down coal train around 1963. The engine carries a 51L, Thornaby, shed plate but had probably just been transferred to Stourton. The sidings to the right of the photograph are the tail end of Holbeck shed yard.

Another Euston to Watford and the north local train sets out from the terminus this time behind a new standard 2-6-4 tank No 80085 also of Bletchley shed. To the left are two of the ineffectual Fowler LMS 2-6-2 tanks which have probably brought in trains of empty coaches from Willesden.

Stirling around 1961–2 with standard 2-6-4 tank No 80061 on an empty stock train passing the former Caledonian locomotive depot. There are three locomotives, probably in store, at the rear of the building a Caledonian 4-4-0 and two 0-6-0s, with an active survivor (NBR J36) next to the diesel shunter above the first coach.

Standard class 4 2-6-0 No 76051 leaves Leeds City station and passes under the Great Northern line from Central at the closed station of Holbeck (High and Low Levels) around 1961. The train is probably bound for Heysham.

for example, took over from their ex-LMS cousins on the cross-Pennine line from Darlington to Penrith and Tebay, where for no very obvious reason they were reckoned to be superior by a quarter of an hour on the through stopping passenger trains. They in turn were supplanted by the standard class 3 2-6-0s when the civil engineer decided that the two Bouch-built viaducts on the route were stronger than previously calculated. This enabled the freight train loadings, largely of coke westbound and iron ore eastbound to be usefully increased.

But undoubtedly the joker in the pack proved to be the class 9F 2-10-0. With 5ft wheels all the indications were that a engine had been produced, suitable for dragging coal and iron ore about in trains without continuous brakes, but not much else, and indeed many of them were successfully used on this type of work. They were busy on the South Wales coal traffic, they largely took over the heavy Toton–Brent coal flow, they monopolised the accelerated Annesley–Woodford 'Windcutter' trains on the old Great Central route, they ran the iron ore in unbraked hoppers from Bidston Dock to John Summers' steelworks at Shotton and in braked hoppers with air-operated doors over the fearsome gradients from Tyne Dock to the now-vanished Consett ironworks. There was a brave experiment in fitting ten new engines with Crosti boilers, the feed heater drum of which was carried under the main barrel with the chimney coming up on the fireman's side

The standard class 3 2-6-2 tanks could perhaps be described as something of an enigma for although forty five of them were built there were many grouping (and pre grouping) locomotives of similar power which could have performed the same duties perfectly. Here No 82026 leaves Leeds Central with an empty stock train for Copley Hill in 1963.

Probably the most successful and certainly the most numerous of the BR standard locomotives was the 9F 2-10-0 of which 251 were built. Eric Treacy found this unusual member of the class No 92167 of Saltley shed (21A) as it headed a Carlisle–Water Orton fast freight just north of Helwith Bridge in the Ribble Valley. This was one of three 9Fs fitted with a mechanical stoker specially for working between Birmingham and Carlisle.

Stoker fitted class 9F 2-10-0 No 92165 of Saltley shed hauling an up fitted freight south of Penrith. The question is raised as to what a specially allocated Saltley engine, presumably on its normal job (a similar train make up, including cattle wagons, to the previous photograph) was doing on the LNW main line. Possibly a diversion for engineering work and/or a derailment.

in front of the firebox. But the potential fuel savings were nullified by the severe corrosion of the heater drum and final 'smokebox', and the extremely dirty cab conditions. After working the Toton–Brent coal trains for 5–6 years, they reverted to conventional form though retaining the non-standard main boiler.

Their free-running characteristics and smooth riding next brought them on to express freight workings. They proved a godsend on the Settle & Carlisle line, with its long and severe gradients and awful winter conditions, and the three engines fitted with mechanical stokers were based at Saltley shed for working the Water Orton–Carlisle and Glasgow fitted freights over this route.

And then, suddenly, they became the flavour of the month for passenger work. At first it was just to help out with easily-timed summer weekend relief trains; such was the confidence they produced, that they began to appear by choice on regular expresses on the English regions (even the Western region succumbed). By 1958 they had been timed at 86mph on the Master Cutler on the Great Central line, and at 90mph on the East Coast main line. Probably drivers did not fully realise the speeds they were reaching, for no speedometers were fitted and the riding was deceptively smooth (so different from the hard, rattling ride of the Britannias and class 5s.) Those small 5ft wheels were being coaxed round at practically the same rate as those of *Mallard* on her 1938 record-breaking run. Clearly enough was enough, and officialdom had no option but to curb these enthusiasms at ground level. In the last years of steam several were based at Bath shed for working summer passenger trains over the severe Somerset & Dorset Joint, when loads soared and double-heading was usual. How those men loved them; they showed that loads of 400 tons and more, unassisted over the Mendips, were well within the capacity of these remarkable engines. The preserved presently working examples, Nos 92203 and 92220 *Evening Star*, will always be a reminder of those halcyon days.

Class 9F 2-10-0 No 92125 passes Wortley North signal box (taken from the Midland's Wortley Junction box) with an up partially fitted freight around 1960. On the left is the Leeds City gas works served by a connection off the Midland line across Canal Street.

BR STANDARD STEAM ENGINES AS CONSTRUCTED

Class 8 4-6-2

Nos.	Built at	Building dates	Region allocated
71000	Crewe	5/54	LM

Authorised as replacement for No. 46202 *Princess Anne*
Total: 1

'Britannia' Class 7 4-6-2

Nos.	Built at	Building dates	Region allocated
70000–70014	Crewe	1/51–6/51	E
70015–70024	,,	6/51–10/51	W
70025–70029	,,	9/52–11/52	W
70030–70034	,,	11/52–12/52	LM
70035–70044	,,	12/52–6/53	E
70045–70049	,,	6/54–7/54	LM
70050–70054	,,	7/54–9/54	Sc

Total: 55

'Clan' Class 6 4-6-2

Nos.	Built at	Building dates	Region allocated
72000–72009	Crewe	12/51–3/52	Sc
72010–72014	,,	Cancelled	S
72015–72024	,,	,,	Sc

Although the allocated names of the BR standard engines are not included in this table, the names selected for these cancelled engines are given for interest.

72010 Hengist	72018 Clan Maclean
72011 Horsa	72019 Clan Douglas
72012 Canute	72020 Clan Gordon
72013 Wildfire	72021 Clan Hamilton
72014 Firebrand	72022 Clan Kennedy
72015 Clan Colquhoun	72023 Clan Lindsay
72016 Clan Graham	72024 Clan Scott
72017 Clan MacDougall	

Total: 10

Class 5 4-6-0

Nos.	Built at	Building dates	Region allocated
73000–73004	Derby	4/51–6/51	LM
73005–73009	,,	6/51–7/51	Sc
73010–73029	,,	9/51–1/52	LM
73030–73039	,,	6/53–9/53	Sc
73040–73049	,,	10/53–12/53	LM
73050–73052	,,	4/54–5/54	S
73053–73054	,,	6/54	LM
73055–73064	,,	6/54–10/54	Sc
73065–73074	,,	10/54–12/54	LM
73075–73079	,,	4/55–5/55	Sc
73080–73089	,,	6/55–9/55	S
73090–73099	,,	10/55–12/55	LM
73100–73109	Doncaster	8/55–1/56	Sc
73110–73119	,,	10/55–12/55	S
73120–73124	,,	1/56–2/56	Sc
73125–73134*	Derby	7/56–10/56	W
73135–73144*	,,	10/56–12/56	LM
73145–73154*	,,	1/57–6/57	Sc
73155–73159	Doncaster	12/56–1/57	E
73160–73171	,,	1/57–5/57	NE

*Fitted with Caprotti valve gear.
Total: 172

Class 4 4-6-0

Nos.	Built at	Building dates	Region allocated
75000–75009	Swindon	5/51–10/51	W
75010–75019	„	11/51–3/52	LM
75020–75029	„	11/53–5/54	W
75030–75049	„	7/53–10/53	LM
75050–75064	„	11/56–7/57	LM
75065–75079	„	8/55–1/56	S
75080–75089	„	Cancelled	E
Total: 80			

Class 4 4-6-0

Nos.	Built at	Building dates	Region allocated
76000–76004	Horwich	12/52	Sc
76005–76019	„	12/52–7/53	S
76020–76024	Doncaster	12/52–1/53	NE
76025–76029	„	10/53–11/53	S
76030–76044	„	11/53–8/54	E
76045–76052	„	3/55–9/56	NE
76053–76069	„	4/55–8/56	S
76070–76074	„	9/56–11/56	Sc
76075–76089	Horwich	12/56–6/57	LM
76090–76099	„	6/57–11/57	Sc
76100–76114	Doncaster	5/57–10/57	Sc
Total: 115			

Class 3 2-6-0

Nos.	Built at	Building dates	Region allocated
77000–77004	Swindon	2/54–3/54	NE
77005–77009	„	3/54–6/54	Sc
77010–77014	„	6/54–7/54	NE
77015–77019	„	7/54–9/54	Sc
Total: 20			

Class 2 2-6-0

Nos.	Built at	Building dates	Region allocated
78000–78009	Darlington	12/52–4/53	W
78010–78019	„	12/53–3/54	NE
78020–78044	„	4/54–12/54	LM
78045–78054	„	10/55–12/55	Sc
78055–78064	„	8/56–11/56	LM
Total: 65			

Class 4 2-6-4T

Nos.	Built at	Building dates	Region allocated
80000–80009	Derby	9/52–12/52	Sc
80010–80019	Brighton	7/51–10/51	S
80020–80030	„	10/51–2/52	Sc
80031–80033	„	2/52–3/52	NE
80034–80053	„	4/52–12/52	LM
80054–80058	Derby	11/54–1/55	Sc
80059–80068	Brighton	3/53–8/53	LM
80069–80080	„	9/53–3/54	E
80081–80095	„	4/54–11/54	LM
80096–80105	„	11/54–4/55	E
80106–80115	Doncaster	10/54–12/54	Sc

BR STANDARD STEAM ENGINES AS CONSTRUCTED
(continued)

80116–80120	Brighton	5/55–7/55	NE
80121–80130	„	8/55–12/55	Sc
80131–80144	„	3/56–9/56	E
80145–80154	„	10/56–3/57	S

Total: 155

Class 3 2-6-2T

Nos.	Built at	Building dates	Region allocated
82000–82009	Swindon	4/52–6/52	W
82010–82019	„	6/52–9/52	S
82020–82029	„	9/54–12/54	S
82030–82034	„	12/54–1/55	W
82035–82044	„	3/55–8/55	W
82045–82054	„	Cancelled	W
82055–82062	„	„	NE

Total: 45

Class 2 2-6-2T

Nos.	Built at	Building dates	Region allocated
84000–84019	Crewe	7/53–10/53	LM
84020–84029	Darlington	3/57–6/57	S

Total: 30

Class 9F 2-10-0 No 92005 simmers in the sunlight and shade of York North shed in 1964–5. Built in 1954 it was transferred from Newport Ebbw Junction to York in September 1963 and remained at 50A until its withdrawal in August 1965.

Class 9F 2-10-0

Nos.	Built at	Building dates	Region allocated
92000–92007	Crewe	1/54–2/54	W
92008–92009	,,	3/54	LM
92010–92014	,,	4/54–5/54	E
92015–92019	,,	9/54–10/54	LM
92020–92029	,,	5/55–7/55	LM
92030–92044	,,	11/54–1/55	E
92045–92059	,,	2/55–10/55	LM
92060–92066	,,	11/55–12/55	NE
92067–92076	,,	12/55–3/56	E
92077–92086	,,	3/56–6/56	LM
92087–92096	,,	8/56–4/57	E
92097–92099	,,	6/56–7/56	NE
92100–92139	,,	8/56–7/57	LM
92140–92149	,,	7/57–10/57	E
92150–92164	,,	10/57–4/58	LM
92165–92167	,,	4/58–6/58	LM
92168–92177	,,	12/57–3/58	E
92178–92202	Swindon	9/57–12/58	E
92203–92220	,,	4/59–3/60	W
92221–92250	Crewe	5/58–12/58	W

Total   251
Total tender engines: 769
Total tank engines: 230

Ten of the class 9F 2-10-0s were built with Crosti boilers – an Italian invention which was not a success in Great Britain as the coal saving was very small and there was serious corrosion of the preheater drum tubes and final smokebox situated below the main boiler. When the smoke was exhausted through the chimney on the right hand side of the boiler it tended to be sucked into the cab making it very dirty. No 92026 of Wellingborough shed (15A) sits in Leeds Holbeck shed in its later days around 1963 with the preheater blanked off and exhausting through the normal chimney.

NAMED TRAINS

The naming of trains grew steadily over the years and by the eve of nationalisation seventy nine trains had been given titles. British Railways in their early days were particularly publicity conscious and more trains than ever before were named, as shown in the list on page 102.

Most named services carried carriage roof boards with the train's title plus the starting and termination stations. BR also added head boards bearing the train's name to many locomotives. These were usually made of aluminium, with the background painted in the appropriate regional colour. Apart from the Great Western's Cheltenham Flyer and the Southern's Golden Arrow, Devon Belle and Bournemouth Belle the only pre-nationalised railway which used locomotive head boards was the LNER.

With the introduction of InterCity 125 sets and the intensive use of locomotive hauled stock on electric and diesel services the use of names declined and the practice of carrying head boards ceased altogether.

Some trains are still named but the prospective passenger has to look very hard to find the title on a relatively small window label.

The Norfolkman. London Liverpool Street c1954 with class 7 4-6-2 No 70001 Lord Hurcomb about to leave with the 09.30 down train. On the left at platform 10 is Thompson L1 2-6-4 tank No 67724 on the empty coaches off the Hook Continental. Both locomotives were built by BR, No 70001 at Crewe in 1951 and No 67724 at Darlington in 1948. This Liverpool Street–Norwich service, calling only at Ipswich, began in 1949.

The South Yorkshireman. One of the two named trains to run over the old Great Central metals (the other was the Master Cutler) heads for Marylebone on the first part of its journey between Bradford and Sheffield behind a dirty Black 5 No 45219 of Low Moor shed (56F). The date would be between May 1957 and 1959.

Tees-Tyne Pullman. An immaculate A4 class 4-6-2 No 60026 Miles Beevor with its 5450 gallon tender piled high with coal heads up the 1 in 107 bank at Belle Isle with the down train in the summer of 1960. This service was introduced by BR as early as 1948 and was intended to be a (slower) Pullman replacement of the pre war Silver Jubilee. By the time Eric Treacy took this photograph the A4s days on the ECML services were numbered as the Deltics were under construction.

The Thanet Belle. Still in Southern Railway livery and numbered 21C154 Battle of Britain class Lord Beaverbrook *leaves London's Victoria station with the down Pullman train in the summer of 1948, its introductory year. The Belle ran to Ramsgate stopping at Whitstable, Herne Bay, Margate and Broadstairs. From 1951 the title was changed to* The Kentish Belle *with the service disappearing on electrification in 1959.*

The Capitals Limited *was introduced to the east coast route in 1949 as a summer non stop service between Kings Cross and Edinburgh Waverley. Class A4 4-6-2 No 60029* Woodcock *heads the up train near Cockburnspath in 1952. The coaches are mostly the Thompson designed Flying Scotsman set of 1947 many in the old 'teak' finish. Based at Kings Cross No 60029 would work the down service one day and the return the next.*

The North Briton was a new name for an old train for there had been a Leeds to Glasgow service via the east coast route for many years before it was so honoured in 1949. Gateshead based A4 No 60019 Bittern (now preserved) leaves Newcastle for Glasgow via Edinburgh Waverley in 1952 or 53.

The Northumbrian. Class A3 Pacific No 60092 Fairway passes Holgate, York with the up train (Newcastle–Kings Cross) probably in the summer of 1950. The engine is in LNER green with the words British Railways in full on the tender and carrying both smokebox number and shed plates but also Heaton on the buffer beam as LNER practice. The train is a mixture of Thompson and Gresley stock with dining facilities provided by a triple articulated restaurant car set.

The White Rose. The up train (the service at the time could hardly be called an express as it took some 4¾ hours to get to Kings Cross calling at all the larger stations en route) leaves Leeds Central c1953 behind class A3 Pacific No 60046 Diamond Jubilee in BR green livery. The engine had recently been converted to left hand drive – easily identifiable by the vacuum ejector pipe just below the handrail.

The West Riding. The 15.45 from Kings Cross, non stop to Wakefield (the BR version of the West Riding Limited) hauled by class A1 Pacific No 60134 Foxhunter heads north through Doncaster c1951. The leading six coaches are the articulated sets from the original pre war train. This scene today is completely different. On the left is a multi-story car park, the station roof has gone and all the running lines are electrified on the 25kv overhead system.

The Heart of Midlothian. The up train (Edinburgh Waverley–London Kings Cross) approaches Chaloners Whin Junction south of York around 1951. The locomotive, an A1 Pacific No 60136 Alcazar although filthy is probably in BR blue livery. The stock is nearly all brand new MkI but the second vehicle is a Gresley brake corridor third and the kitchen car in the centre of the train is a Thompson design built by BR.

The non stop Kings Cross service to Edinburgh changed its name from The Capitals Limited to The Elizabethan to honour the Queen's Coronation. Eric Treacy captured the busy scene on a summer morning at Edinburgh Waverley in 1961, the last year of the Gresley Pacifics on this exacting working. No 60009 Union of South Africa pulls out of Platform 10 prompt to time (the North British Hotel clock was kept permanently two minutes fast!) at 09.45 whilst in the adjacent platform Peak class 45 1Co-Co1 D11 waits at the head of 1M88, The Waverley, for St Pancras.

The Red Rose. Rebuilt Patriot class 4-6-0 No 45521 Rhyl comes to a stand just south of Crewe station with the down train sometime in the mid 1950s. It was stopped by a red signal on the gantry which Eric Treacy had climbed to take the photograph! The Red Rose was introduced in 1951 and received a set of the newly introduced MkI stock seen here in its original colour scheme.

The Elizabethan's last year. The up train departs from Edinburgh Waverley in the summer of 1962 behind Deltic No D9006 not yet named Fife and Forfar Yeomanry (1964). This was the only year when the train ran using Deltics as motive power and a stop at Newcastle became necessary to change crews. On the right class 45 No D18 has a twenty minute wait before setting off with the 10.05 departure for St Pancras.

The Shamrock. Peak class 1Co-Co1 No D9 Snowdon leaves Euston with the down train in 1960. The Shamrock was a late afternoon non-stop Euston–Liverpool Lime Street service named in 1954. Early in 1962 all ten members of the class moved to Toton where they were employed on freight duties.

The Talisman. With the clock showing 08.32 the morning Talisman heads south from Edinburgh for Kings Cross behind class A4 Pacific No 60009 Union of South Africa *sometime in 1960. No 60009 was one of the more fortunate A4s ending its days of service on the Glasgow–Aberdeen section of the old Caledonian Railway. It is now preserved.*

The Talisman. The up train emerging from Calton Hill tunnel Edinburgh hauled by Deltic Co-Co No D9018 Ballymoss *in 1962. This was the first year of Deltic haulage reducing the time from London to Edinburgh to six hours. The Talisman was introduced in 1956 as a 16.00 departure from both King Cross and Edinburgh; a year later a morning service was added.*

The Caledonian. Camden based Duchess No 46239 City of Chester passing its home depot with the down train in the summer of 1957. This six hour forty minute service between Euston and Glasgow was introduced in 1957 stopping only at Carlisle. The Caledonian left Euston at 16.15 (to rival the Eastern Region's Talisman), the southbound train departing Glasgow at 08.30. From 1958 the service was extended to provide a morning and an afternoon train in each direction. No 46239 is in Brunswick green livery with the earlier BR symbol and the coaches are in maroon livery (this combination is often a good indicator of a date c1957, assisted here by the fact that the locomotive's smokebox was rebuilt from 'semi streamlined' form in 1957).

PRINCIPAL NAMED TRAINS INTRODUCED BY BR

1948	THE NORFOLKMAN	Liverpool St.–Norwich
1948	SOUTH YORKSHIREMAN	Marylebone–Bradford
1948	TEES-TYNE PULLMAN	Newcastle–Kings Cross
1948	THANET BELLE	Victoria–Ramsgate
ran 1948–1950 until renamed (see Kentish Belle)		
1949	THE CAPITALS LIMITED	Kings Cross–Edinburgh
ran until 1952 (see Elizabethan)		
1949	THE FENMAN	Hunstanton–Liverpool St.
1949	THE NORTH BRITON	Leeds–Glasgow Queen St.
1949	THE NORTHUMBRIAN	Kings Cross–Newcastle
1949	WEST RIDING	Bradford, Leeds–Kings Cross
1949	THE WHITE ROSE	Kings Cross–Leeds, Bradford
1950	THE BROADSMAN	Cromer–Liverpool St.
1950	THE EASTERLING	Liverpool St.–Yarmouth (Summer only)
1950	THE INTER CITY	Paddington–Wolverhampton
1950	RED DRAGON	Paddington–Carmarthen
1950	THE TYNESIDER	Newcastle–Kings Cross
overnight service		
1950	THE MIDLANDER	Euston–Birmingham–Wolverhampton
1951	THE HEART OF MIDLOTHIAN	Kings Cross–Edinburgh
1951	KENTISH BELLE	Victoria–Ramsgate
formerly Thanet Belle		
1951	THE MERCHANT VENTURER	Paddington–Bristol
1951	THE RED ROSE	Euston–Liverpool Lime St.
1951	THE ROYAL WESSEX	Waterloo–Weymouth
1952	THE CORNISHMAN	Wolverhampton–Penzance
1952	NORTHERN IRISHMAN	Euston–Stranraer Hbr.
1953	THE ELIZABETHAN	Kings Cross–Edinburgh
formerly Capitals Limited		
1953	MAN OF KENT	Charing Cross–Sandwich via Folkestone
1953	PEMBROKE COAST EXPRESS	Paddington–Pembroke Dock
1954	EMERALD ISLE EXPRESS	Euston–Holyhead
1954	THE SHAMROCK	Liverpool Lime St.–Euston
1955	SOUTH WALES PULLMAN	Paddington–Swansea
1956	CAPITALS UNITED	Cardiff–Paddington
1956	THE TALISMAN	Kings Cross–Edinburgh
1957	THE CALEDONIAN	Glasgow Central–Euston
1957	THE CATHEDRALS EXPRESS	Paddington–Worcester, Hereford
1957	THE MAYFLOWER	Plymouth–Paddington
1957	THE ROYAL DUCHY	Penzance–Paddington
1957	THE FAIR MAID	Kings Cross–Perth
1957	THE WAVERLEY	St. Pancras–Edinburgh
1958	THE ESSEX COAST EXPRESS	Liverpool St.–Clacton
1959	THE ROBIN HOOD	St. Pancras–Nottingham
1960	BIRMINGHAM PULLMAN	Paddington–Wolverhampton
1960	BRISTOL PULLMAN	Paddington–Bristol
1960	MIDLAND PULLMAN	St. Pancras–Manchester Central
1964	THE GOLDEN HIND	Plymouth–Paddington
1964	THE NORTH EASTERN	Kings Cross–Newcastle
1966	MANCHESTER PULLMAN	Euston–Manchester Piccadilly
1966	LIVERPOOL PULLMAN	Euston–Liverpool Lime St.
1966	NIGHT LIMITED	Euston–Glasgow Central
1966	NIGHT LIMITED	
overnight service		
1974	THE CLANSMAN	Euston–Inverness

The Waverley. The Midland route services from London St Pancras to Scotland were no stranger to named trains the LMS running both The Thames Clyde and The Thames Forth expresses. In 1957 the latter once again became a named train this time The Waverley running as always over the Settle–Carlisle route thence over North British metals to Edinburgh. Jubilee class 4-6-0 No 45608 Gibraltar passes Hellifield with the down train c1959 the only other LMS artifact being the dining car. The Waverley ceased to run with the closure of the NBR Waverley route in 1969.

Manchester Pullman. Platform 14 of the new Euston station in 1967 with this special business train, introduced the previous year, awaiting homegoing passengers at 17.45 on a weekday evening. Originally there were two trains a day in each direction (later extended to three); this is the 18.00 down departure. The train consists of MkII Pullman cars built at Derby in 1966.

Manchester Pullman motive power. Built by BR at Doncaster works 25kv electric locomotive class AL6 (later 86) No E3137 awaits departure at Euston. The locomotive is in BR electric blue livery with white window surrounds and cab roof and a small yellow panel; it has raised metal numbers a BTC crest and is dual fitted although the coaches are vacuum braked.

THE ALTERNATIVES TO STEAM

Fifty-two 0-6-0 diesel electric shunting locomotives, forty diesel mechanical railcars, and one brand new Co-Co main line diesel electric locomotive. Such was the inventory when British Railways was born in January 1948.

Forty-four of the shunters came from the LMS, which had been experimenting with diesel power in this field since 1932. By 1941 they had standardised a design with two nose-suspended motors and the 350hp English Electric 6KT engine. Because of high availability, single manning and scope for intensive utilisation there was a forward building programme for this locomotive. This type, with only minor alterations, formed the basis of a BR standard engine and many hundreds were subsequently built. Its economic attraction ensured that with the 1955 Modernisation Plan they totally replaced steam shunting engines.

But the 6KT diesel engine was very conservatively rated, and even in

The pair of H.G. Ivatt/English Electric designed Co-Cos Nos 10000 (built just prior to nationalisation) and 10001 (1948) double head the up Royal Scot through the Lune Gorge in 1958 or 59. They were built using English Electric 1600hp engines giving a power classification of only 5P5F and were therefore used in multiple on heavier duties. Both locomotives are in Brunswick green livery and carry a light blue-grey band. Soon after this date all the top WCML expresses were limited to eight coaches and given the same London–Glasgow timings with one stop to Carlisle.

Nos 10000 and 10001 take the down Royal Scot through Carnforth on 16 July 1957. Carnforth shed and station are in the background showing a scene vastly different from today. The shed would be fully operational for over another decade, the goods yard is busy and the whole of the station still in use. Today the WCML is electrified, Carnforth shed is now used as a tourist/preservation centre and the main line platforms of the station are closed. No 10000 was withdrawn in 1963 and No 10001 three years later.

extended form not suitable for main line work. At the end of World War II the LMS had sent three of its officers to the USA to study diesel traction there. As a result of their report, discussions were opened with English Electric Co on the power equipment for two diesel electric main line locomotives, capable of working in multiple. The engine selected was a turbocharged 1600hp unit and the LMS announced early in 1947 that two Co-Co locomotives were to be built at Derby. The first, No 10000 was completed just before nationalisation but No 10001 did not appear until seven months into the BR era (see table). They were attractive machines with end noses fitted with doors to give a walkway between locomotives, a feature which subsequently proved superfluous. They worked on the London Midland and Southern regions on both passenger and freight turns, but in multiple only briefly on the Royal Scot train.

Ever a steam man, Treacy seemed pleased enough to see their black shiny livery, offset by a broad aluminium waistband and numbers, working over the Lancaster and Carlisle section. So, of course, were the enginemen! But their availability was only fair and the lack of dedicated maintenance facilities did nothing to help; turbocharger failures were particularly troublesome. Their lives of eighteen and fifteen years provided valuable experience for developing later classes.

The LMS had also announced at the time a smaller Bo-Bo locomotive for branch and cross-country work. The machine was a long time in gestation, and as No 10800, was not delivered until 1950. In its nine year life in this form it wandered extensively about the country, spending some time working on the Oxford–Cambridge line. It proved seriously underpowered for effective use and suffered a number of technical problems. It was later sold to Brush and rebuilt for use as a testbed.

Of the diesel railcars taken over, all but three had been built for or by the GWR. Starting with a single car built by AEC in 1933, using a standard 130hp bus engine and transmission, the design had developed through single cars with twin engines, enabling them to handle a trailer coach, to twin sets with buffet facility. Interestingly, all power maintenance was carried out on contract by the manufacturers. On certain routes they proved to have inadequate capacity for their commercial success, and had to be replaced by locomotive hauled trains. Apart from these vehicles, GWR experience was confined to a single 350hp diesel electric shunter.

The GWR seemed to have no diesel locomotive ambitions, and instead, remarkably perhaps, leaned towards the gas turbine. A project was initiated with Metropolitan-Vickers to build a locomotive with a gas turbine derived from the firm's aircraft units and running on gas oil. Shortly after, another order was placed with the Swiss firm of Brown-Boveri for a single locomotive, similar to one already running on the Swiss Federal Railways, the turbine being based more on industrial types and using a heavier residual fuel oil. The gas turbine could not offer the thermal efficiency of the diesel engine, but its high power weight ratio and modest maintenance and lubricating oil needs were factors in its favour. The Swiss built No 18000 was delivered in February 1950 and the Metro-Vick No 18100 in December 1951.

Swiss built Brown Boveri gas turbine A1A-A1A locomotive No 18000 leaves Paddington with an express for Cheltenham Spa c1951. The livery carried is black with a silver band similar to the pair of LMS diesel electrics. After numerous trials and satisfactory service for a number of years the locomotive was withdrawn in December 1960. It was sold back to the manufacturers in the mid 1960s and still exists stored at Vienna.

Mechanical trouble dogged the Brown-Boveri locomotive in its early years, but availability gradually improved, with the engine working

mainly between Paddington and Bristol. On test on the South Devon banks its performance was impressive, but *overall* thermal efficiency for a day's duty was less than 7%, little better than that of a steam locomotive; its high power was seldom called for, and at part load the turbine efficiency plummeted. At the end of 1960 it was withdrawn and ultimately sold back to its builders for further research work. The Metro-Vick locomotive put in a lot of work on the Bristol and Plymouth routes, with few problems – though it was carefully nursed by the maker's staff. In 1959 it was returned to Metro-Vick and converted into a 25kv electric locomotive No E1000 for driver training and equipment testing on the newly electrified Manchester/Liverpool–Crewe routes, and for minor research work, before being scrapped in 1972.

An interesting side effect of the use of these two locomotives was that their prolific exhaust scoured the soot and dirt from tunnel roofs, bridges and station awnings; the civil engineer was thought to prefer more conventional methods of cleaning!

Even then gas turbine propulsion continued to attract locomotive engineers. Nos 18000 and 18100 had both used electrical transmission to accommodate the high turbine speeds, but English Electric resolved to test a simple mechanical transmission, building in 1961 a loco-motive, GT3, with a 2700hp turbine and looking more like a streamlined 4-6-0 steam tender engine than anything else. It performed well in tests, but had no place in BR's modernisation plans and within two years went back to English Electric for scrapping.

Since the 1920s the Southern Railway tended to be thought of as an electric railway on which steam played a subsidiary role. But the main routes to the West of England and to the Kent Coast were still steam hauled and likely to remain so for the foreseeable future. To meet post war conditions the Southern began talking to English Electric in 1946, even before the LMS did so, and also adopted the 16SVT engine, though by 1950, when the first of three locomotives, No 10201, emerged from Ashford works it had been uprated to 1750hp. No 10202 followed in June 1951. Bulleid adopted the fairly novel 1Co-Co1 wheel arrangement. Their appearance did not compare with the ex LMS twins, being very *boxy* with vertical cab fronts and no noses.

After initial tests and various modifications, they settled down on West of England trains. The last locomotive of the trio came from Brighton Works in March 1954, with the English Electric engine further uprated to develop 2000hp. It was not long, however, before all three were transferred to the West Coast main line; for a time Nos 10201/2 (when both were available) ran in multiple on the Royal Scot as far as Carlisle, and 10203 with its extra power ran the train single handed. Treacy made their acquaintance amongst the northern fells, but was unable to coax much life from them for his pictures – they looked too much like another coach for that. But their appearances became fewer, and they gravitated to less important work until in the winter of 1962/3 they were withdrawn. However, unlike the standard steam locomotives which reflected much LMS practice, the four axle bogie design of the Southern diesels lived on in BR's Modernisation Plan of 1955, though not without mechanical problems.

The last company to take a positive initiative was the LNER. The authorities at Kings Cross, ever near the breadline, and with plenty of

high-powered steam locomotives were slower to succumb to the diesel lure. However in mid 1947 the LNER Board authorised a scheme for the complete dieselisation of the Kings Cross–Edinburgh passenger services. For a railway with only four diesel electric shunters just two years old, it was, to say the least, rather ambitious! Twenty five Co-Co diesel electric locomotives of 1600hp each – one detects the hand of English Electric here – working in pairs would displace thirty-two Pacific steam locomotives to other services. But with hindsight the assessment was flawed in assuming an unrealistically high availability of the diesel locomotives. Tenders were obtained from half-a-dozen firms, but under BR oversight no further action was taken. There were already five comparable machines running or on order with which to assess the problems!

One more diesel locomotive must be covered to complete the picture. Just prior to nationalisation, H.G. Ivatt at Derby was approached by Colonel L.F.R. Fell, who had developed a novel form of mechanical transmission for locomotives. It showed sufficient promise for Ivatt to get authority to design and build a mainline locomotive on this system for Fell Developments Limited.

No 10100 emerged in January 1951 with features like none that had been seen before. It could be described in steam terms as a 4-8-4 with outside frames and coupling rods. There were long nose sections, each holding two supercharged engines. The power from these was transmitted through fluid couplings to a central gearbox, which was flexibly coupled to the two centre axles. By a system of differentials

Beattock summit c1958 with the up train double headed by Southern Region 1Co-Co1 diesel electrics Nos 10201 and 10202. These two locomotives were built at Ashford under the direction of O.V. Bulleid in 1950–51 using English Electric engines and electrical equipment. After working over the Southern Region both were transferred to the LMR where they worked WCML duties. They too were classified 5P5F (1750hp) and used in the same manner as the LMS prototypes.

Carlisle around 1956–7 with the later and more powerful Southern Region diesel electric locomotive No 10203. This was built at Brighton works in 1954 incorporating a 2000hp English Electric engine, giving it the enhanced power classification 7. Contrary to Nos 10201 and 10202 this locomotive was not built with gangway doors. All three were finally withdrawn at the end of 1963 after a period in store.

and clutches, the four engines could be brought on line progressively to increase speed, full power being available from about 25mph. The superchargers were separately driven by an auxiliary engine to control main engine torque over a wide speed range.

After proving trials, No 10100 was employed almost entirely on the St Pancras–Manchester Central route of the London Midland Region. This was rather off Treacy's beaten track, and the Fell's whirling coupling rods seem to have eluded him; he would surely have approved this reversion to steam practice. Alas, the locomotive proved unreliable, and spent lengthy spells in the works at Derby; during one of these in 1955 the centre sections of the coupling rods were removed to produce what *appeared* to be a 4-4-4-4 (though the two centre axles were still coupled through the gearbox). Finally, in October 1958, the Fell was severely damaged by an engine fire in Manchester Central Station and never ran again.

Still by the end of 1954, when the final touches were being applied to the forthcoming Modernisation Plan, BR was operating seven mainline diesel and two gas turbine locomotives, together with over 300 diesel shunters. About 19,000 steam locomotives were still in service. The plan, the fruits of which will be dealt with in the following chapters, required some 2,500 diesel locomotives – the gas turbine alternative had been rejected – in addition to more electrification of suburban and main line routes. But the plan failed to recognise the need for locomotives of high power without multiple working; only twenty eight of the first 174 locomotives ordered were of higher power than 1250hp. Two diesel engines were actively competing for the top of the market; the English Electric 16SVT, already installed in No 10203 at 2000hp, and under further development, got ten of the *initial* orders in class 40s while the Sulzer 12LDA28 had been ordered for ten class 44s at 2300hp and was being uprated next to 2500hp. The remaining locomotives needed two diesel engines to provide 2000hp. Notwithstanding the bias towards moderate power, there would clearly be a large market for locomotives of high power which could work the hardest jobs single handed. In the event, four one-off prototypes were produced to tap this potential.

First in the field was English Electric in 1955. The Napier Deltic engine, a lightweight opposed piston unit which had been proved in fast naval patrol boats, was in production in 18 cylinder form and rated at 1650hp. Two of these engines, with electric transmission, were installed in a Co-Co demonstrator locomotive numbered DP1 (though it never actually carried this number), the weight of the locomotive in working order being no more than 106 tons. Built by English Electric in Preston, it was loaned to British Rail for service testing, and looked striking in its livery of powder blue, offset by aluminium mouldings, and with yellow 'whisker' markings on each nose. For three years, *Deltic* was allocated to Edge Hill shed, though it ran dynamometer car trials on the Skipton–Carlisle route in 1956. There were teething troubles with the engines, which did not take kindly to the constant load variations inherent in railway work, but these were partly resolved and the locomotive settled down on Liverpool–Euston services. What more could Treacy wish for? Here was a locomotive which stood out from its background in any photograph, in sunlight or overcast weather. The smooth, high-pitched engine roar on which the scream of

A further photograph of No 10203 in dark green livery bearing the second BR emblem heading a down express, probably the down Royal Scot, through the Lune Gorge near Tebay c1959.

110

The most successful prototype diesel locomotive was the Deltic built by English Electric with two Napier 18 cylinder Deltic engines. This began running trials in November 1955 and worked service trains from the summer of 1956 over the London Midland Region and later on the Eastern. After nearly six years of satisfactory running the prototype was withdrawn and transferred to the Science Museum in April 1963. It is now on permanent display.

The following three pictures were caught by Eric Treacy's camera.

The up Merseyside Express 10.10 Liverpool Lime St. to Euston passing Edge Hill in the spring of 1957. This is the first visible sign of modernisation but the majority of the railway scene is much as it had been for the past fifty, sixty, seventy years with loose coupled freight trains and steam shunting locos.

the turbochargers was superimposed, made it quite distinctive. He thought it worth recording at both ends of its runs.

But other eyes besides Treacy's were cast in *Deltic's* direction. The Eastern and North Eastern regions had dusted off the 1947 dieselisation proposals and recast them to include Leeds and Newcastle workings. Here was a locomotive which would avoid multipling and substantially speed up the East Coast services. In March 1958 twenty-two similar locomotives were ordered from English Electric – the future class 55. In the meantime, *Deltic* was transferred to Hornsey shed early in 1959 for extended trials, following which it went into regular service to evaluate its reliability. Throughout all this running it was in the hands of English Electric staff for inspection and maintenance. But in March 1963 a serious engine failure took place, and the demonstrator was withdrawn, its objective successfully achieved. It is now in the Science Museum, London.

The firm of Brush at Loughborough in the late 1950s had a modest involvement in the dieselisation programme, but the Deltic order seemed to spur them into action. If a single demonstrator could get an order such as this, then Brush could likewise get into the market. In 1959, after discussion with BR, the construction of a 2800hp diesel electric Co-Co locomotive was authorised. This was completed in September 1961 as No D0280, named *Falcon* after the works which

Another Liverpool–Euston express, probably the 14.10 as it does not carry a headboard, passing Edge Hill locomotive depot coaling plant in the autumn of 1957.

At the top of Camden bank on the last lap into Euston. Judging by the direction of the sun this must be the 14.10 Manxman (only named in the summer) from Liverpool.

built it, and turned out in a startling livery of lime green and chestnut brown. Because no suitable single diesel engine of sufficient power was yet available, two Maybach 12 cylinder engines, similar to those used in the class 42 diesel hydraulics, rated at 1350hp (though with capability for 1440hp) were fitted.

After tests on the Western Region it returned to Brush for modifications which lasted a year. It was then sent to Darnall shed for a further seven months of testing on both passenger and freight diagrams, followed by another lengthy spell at Loughborough works. From the beginning of 1965 *Falcon*, now in Brunswick green, went to Bristol Bath Road shed, where it was maintained by BR with Brush involvement in electrical repairs. In 1971 after purchase by British Rail and overhaul it emerged in blue and renumbered 1200. It put in another four years work, mainly on Port Talbot–Llanwern iron ore workings, before withdrawal in October 1975. With such a gypsy existence it is not surprising that Treacy never caught up with *Falcon*.

The year 1962 saw the appearance of two new high powered demonstrator locomotives. By now an order had been placed for the first twenty class 47 machines from Brush, but it was felt that there was enough business for other manufacturers too. First to see the light of day, by a whisker, was English Electric's DP2; it featured the bogies and some of the body of a production class 55 Deltic in which was installed the latest version of the trusty 16 cylinder engine which had first powered Nos 10000/1, now uprated to produce 2700hp.

DP2 entered service on the West Coast main line, where it quickly earned a reputation for reliability. The enginemen and maintenance staff were enthusiastic – at last a manufacturer had got it right with a higher-powered locomotive. After a year it was sent to Finsbury Park and started to build up mileage fast on the East Coast, often working Deltic diagrams. Meanwhile, English Electric were working to develop electronic control systems, and in 1966 DP2 was called into Vulcan Foundry – who had built it originally – to be fitted with this equipment. After very satisfactory testing, including restarts of heavy trains on Shap, DP2 returned to Finsbury Park late in 1966 and resumed its high mileage diagrams. But on 31 July 1967, while working the 12.00 Kings Cross–Edinburgh, it collided with derailed Presflo wagons near Thirsk, and was seriously damaged. DP2 never ran again, but it had served its purpose.

Hard on the heels of DP2 came the second (and in appearance much more spectacular) locomotive, the product of an alliance between Birmingham Railway Carriage, Sulzer and Associated Electrical Industries. No D0260 was based on the Sulzer 12LDA28C engine, also used in the class 47 and now boosted to 2750hp. The locomotive was much lighter than the comparable class 45 and ran on three axle bogies. It was called *Lion* and emerged in a striking livery of white with gold lining. Alas, its life did not match its appearance. After testing on the Western Region from Wolverhampton Stafford Road shed, it ran into technical problems which necessitated modification by the builders. After further tests it moved to Finsbury Park, and it was in this phase that it paraded before Treacy's lens in the Leeds Central–Wakefield area on the Yorkshire Pullman, standing out like a ghost against some grimy backgrounds. But it was beset with power unit problems – as was the class 47 until the engine was derated – and late in 1963, still less than two years old, it returned to its builders. By now BRC&W was in severe financial straits, and with no early prospect of being adopted by BR it was summarily scrapped.

Meanwhile BR had found what it was looking for in the Brush design class 47 with Sulzer engine. This was in mass production from 1962 until 1967, and the market for an alternative locomotive in this power range had virtually dried up. When a new prototype appeared nearly six years later, it was again from the Brush stable, now part of the Hawker Siddeley Group. No HS4000, named *Kestrel*, represented a quantum leap in installed power; the diesel engine was a 16 cylinder Sulzer 16LVA24 in vee formation rather than the usual double-bank layout, rated at 4000hp. It was carried on a Co-Co chassis, but weighed no less than 133 tonnes, the axleload making it unacceptable to BR for high speed. For twelve months it ran various heavy haulage trials, meeting all expectations, and then was rebogied for passenger service with some weight reduction. Now it worked from Finsbury Park on a Kings Cross–Newcastle service, resplendent in its unusual brown and yellow livery. After eight months on this work, followed by an engine overhaul – it was not a happy power unit – *Kestrel* returned to Shirebrook and more coal haulage. Early in 1971 the engine was withdrawn for modifications before being sold and shipped to the USSR, a rare export opportunity. Treacy never caught up with this heavyweight with sheer brute strength.

So this prototype phase in BR's modernisation saga covered fifteen locomotives of twelve different designs. Their influence on ordering within the Modernisation Plan was patchy. The two LMS and three SR locomotives with English Electric engines paved the way for class 40, one of the more successful designs in the fleet, though ponderous and low powered. *Deltic* led directly to class 55, which, at a cost, revolutionised East Coast passenger running. And DP2 was the forerunner of the class 50, though something was lost in the development. The remainder got nowhere.

One prototype which was not taken up by BR was Lion *built by the Birmingham Railway Carriage & Wagon Co in 1962. For a month or so prior to withdrawal in October 1963* Lion *was on loan to the Eastern Region and used on the Yorkshire Pullman between Leeds Central and Kings Cross. It is seen here leaving Leeds Central in September 1963.*

English Electric prototype DP2 a 2700hp Co-Co emerged from the Vulcan Foundry, Newton-le-Willows in 1962 and ran extensively on BR's London Midland and Eastern Regions proving to be a very successful locomotive. DP2 is seen passing Portobello East signalbox with the down relief Flying Scotsman c1964, in its original livery of plain Brunswick green with small yellow panel. The locomotive was withdrawn in 1967 after suffering collision damage in the Thirsk accident of 31 July 1967. DP2's success lead to the production of the class 50 fleet, indeed the engine from DP2 was reused in D400.

PROTOTYPE LOCOMOTIVES

Year Built	Builder	Running Number/Name	Wheel Arrgt.	Power Unit	HP	Transmission	Weight tons	Max Speed mph	
Diesel									
1947/8	LMS/BR Derby	10000/1	Co-Co	English Electric 16SVT	1600	EE electric	131	93	
1950	N British	10800	Bo-Bo	Paxman 16PHXL	827	BTH electric	70	70	Rebuilt by Brush for experimental purposes
1950/1	BR Ashford	10201/2	1-Co-Co-1	English Electric 16SVT	1750	EE electric	135	90	
1951	BR Derby	10100	4-8-4	4 x Paxman 12RPH	2400	Vulcan Sinclair fluid couplings and Fell patent gearbox	120	78	
1954	BR Brighton	10203	1-Co-Co-1	English Electric 16SVT Mk2	2000	EE electric	132	90	
1955	EE Preston	*Deltic*	Co-Co	2 x Napier Deltic D18–25	3300	EE electric	106	90	Max speed later increased to 105mph
1961	Brush	D0280 *Falcon*	Co-Co	2 x Maybach MD655	2700	Brush electric	115	100	
1962	EE/Vulcan	DP2	Co-Co	English Electric 16SVT	2700	EE electric	105	90	
1962	BRC&W	D0260 *Lion*	Co-Co	Sulzer 12LDA28C	2750	AEI electric	114	100	
1968	Brush	HS4000 *Kestrel*	Co-Co	Sulzer 16LVA24	4000	Brush electric	133	125	
Gas Turbine									
1950	Brown Boveri	18000	A1A–A1A	Brown Boveri	2500	Brown Boveri electric	115	90	
1951	MetroVick	18100	Co-Co	Metropolitan Vickers	3000	MetroVick electric	129	90	
1961	EE/Vulcan	GT3	4-6-0	English Electric EM276	2700	Mechanical	123	90	

No D0260 Lion passes Copley Hill shed with the up Yorkshire Pullman in September 1963. Eric Treacy must have been impressed by the looks of this type 4 machine as he took about a dozen pictures of it during trials over Eastern Region metals.

THE FRUITS OF MODERNISATION

1 – The Plan and its Multiple Units

It was in January 1955 that the British Transport Commission (the British Railways Board did not come into being until 1963) announced its fifteen-year plan for the modernisation and re-equipment of British Railways. It was comprehensive, and was estimated to cost £1,240 million. It would see the total disappearance of steam traction; new steam locomotive construction for passenger work would cease with the 1956 building programme, and for freight within a few years. Steam had to go because of the increasing shortage of large coal, pollution and cleanliness, increasing staff shortages for its servicing, and its poor acceleration prospects. Limited main line electrification would come where traffic levels warranted, and suburban electric working would spread; where these could not be justified, diesel locomotives and multiple units would be brought in as fast as possible. The figures quoted were astronomical; a thousand electric main line locomotives, 3600 electric multiple unit vehicles, about 4600 diesel multiple unit vehicles and 2500 main line diesel locomotives. The bill for these traction changes would be about £345 million at prices then current (it would be more than £3 billion in 1990).

Against the background of existing operations it was a turning point indeed. From the dismal immediate post war years there had been a gradual renaissance in passenger services, with prewar speeds largely regained; fifty-nine trains daily were timed at over 60mph start to stop, the fastest being the Bristolian at just over 67mph. But there had been little *fundamental* change in thirty years. Superannuated 4-4-0s led three non-gangwayed coaches on tours of little-used country stations, small tank engines pottered about on single line branches with single coaches, shunted milk depots and picked up the occasional horsebox. The local freight trip radiated from marshalling yards in vast numbers, dropping a couple of wagons of domestic coal here, collecting a wagon of cattle there. Containers were of wood for a three ton payload, making the intermodal transfer by courtesy of a vintage yard crane and chain slings. Treacy recorded it all the time as a backcloth for his hard-working steam locomotives. And yet limited modernisation *was* going on. Suburban electrification *was* spreading, albeit slowly; the first diesel units, prototypes for the future, were already in service. A handful of main line diesel locomotives were shakily gaining experience to guide future orders. The 1500v dc Manchester–Sheffield–Wath electric main line was up and running, and between Lancaster, Morecambe and Heysham, ac overhead electrification at industrial frequency was on trial. So what really emerged in the Modernisation Plan was not so much a technological breakthrough, more a massive stepping up of the pace of change already taking place. But as Gerry Fiennes wrote later; 'we had made the basic error of buying our tools before doing our homework on defining the job.'

The Modernisation Plan showed all the signs of having been cobbled together in a great hurry at someone's bidding from on high, with

To the left of the picture is one of the very first Derby 'Lightweight' dmus, to the right the last design of LNER Pacific the A1; built only five years apart, neither enjoyed a long life. The scene is Leeds Central station c1955. The dmu (driving motor composite No E79502 leading) is a two-car set for Bradford Exchange whilst A1 Pacific No 60123 H.A. Ivatt is waiting to head the Queen of Scots south to Kings Cross; it was officially withdrawn in October 1962 having been involved in an accident at Offord in August. E79502 was withdrawn in 1964 having completed less than ten years service.

Soon after their introduction in late 1954 and a month after their allocation to this route Eric Treacy photographed this Derby 'Lightweight' set leaving Keswick for Workington; it was February 1955. The train consists of a driving motor brake second M79009 and a driving trailer composite with lavatory. This batch was adapted for the restricted clearances over the Maryport & Carlisle line with bars fitted across the passenger droplights. It was hoped that the introduction of dmus would provide a healthy future for the CK&P but Keswick became a terminus out of Penrith in 1966; even this was withdrawn in March 1972.

119

A Derby 'Lightweight' dmu leaves Braithwaite for Penrith and Carlisle in 1965–6, just before closure of the Keswick–Workington section, in April 1966. The leading car No 79124 is an early one and it was withdrawn (as non standard) towards the end of the 1960s. Freight traffic had already been withdrawn (June 1964) as shown by the derelict sidings.

figures plucked off the ceiling, without looking fully at the implications of the changeover in traction. The new BR standard class 2MT 2-6-2T was introduced in July 1953 and in February 1954 the first BR standard class 3MT 2-6-0 followed: Four months later the first new diesel trains entered service in West Yorkshire, and thus began to take away the very type of work for which these smaller steam locomotives had just been built.

Attempts to provide the right diesel unit for branch line and secondary services have a long history. In Britain the Great Western Railway had been in the lead, with the LMS following a long way behind with its three Leyland railbuses working in Lancashire and later in Scotland. The other two companies showed little interest. Indeed, when the issue was raised in the House of Commons in 1952 the Ministry of Transport replied that limitations on BR's investment programme were preventing them from ordering diesel railcars, but a committee had been examining the subject and its findings were under review.

It was at this time that ACV Limited, a holding company including AEC and Park Royal Coachwork, produced a novel three-car diesel train for BR to try out; it comprised two four wheeled power cars, each with a standard AEC 125hp bus engine driving one axle through a fluid flywheel and four speed epicyclic gearbox, with a four wheeled trailer between. The austere body styling certainly did no credit to Park Royal, having a faintly Colonel Stephens air about it. Maximum speed was 45mph. After demonstration between Marylebone and Princes Risborough the train was used for a time on the Harrow–Belmont and

In 1956 Derby produced a diesel-electric multiple unit test bed incorporating 450hp underfloor mounted Paxman engines. The two-car set consisted of LMS open brake seconds, converted to include a drivers cab at the brake ends, mounted on motor bogies from Euston–Watford electric units. The set ran extensive trials over the LMR latterly over the Settle–Carlisle route, where it is seen here coming off Ribblehead viaduct into the station c1957. The livery is standard dmu green with cream lining.

A Metro-Cammell dmu (class 101) heads out of Carlisle on a Newcastle service c1956–7. These sets were then new (introduced in 1956 – some four-car sets for the NE Region having buffet facilities) and replaced classes such as the D49 4-4-0s on secondary services. The 101s were built in large numbers and used in two, three and four-car formations. No E50175, the leading vehicle is a motor composite.

Watford–St. Albans branches. Its riding left much to be desired, and flange wear proved to be heavy.

Following the BR review, a decision to start building diesel railcars was taken late in 1952. The concept was of a two coach unit of motor coach and trailer built in light alloy, though on heavily graded lines two power cars could be used. Up to four units could be multipled. Each power car would have two underfloor horizontal diesel engines, and suitable units were already proved in road transport. The first units went into service in 1954 on the steeply graded lines between Leeds Central and Bradford/Harrogate and 125hp engines drove through a torque converter and every vehicle was powered. The next units, of power car and trailer, were fitted with fluid flywheels and four speed epicyclic gearboxes and went to West Cumberland, for the winter of 1954/5. Further sets followed for Birmingham, Lincolnshire, East Anglia and the Newcastle area.

Commercially they were an instant success. Passengers who had grown up to accept grubby and frowsty coaches, took to the new trains with enthusiasm – and told their friends. They were comfortable in bus-style, though their rather unreliable oil fired heaters could work up a powerful fume-tainted fug. Timings were sharpened up and from some seats, there was the added bonus of seeing where you were going and watching the driver at work. Loadings rose, and at peak times brought

Skipton South Junction with a multiple unit train made up of three two-car class 108s (dating from 1958) entering the station c1960 with a service from Leeds or Bradford. Note the Midland wooden signal post with LMS replacement upper quadrant arms.

problems; inflexible formation caused considerable standing, and with crush loadings the light alloy body distorted sufficiently to jam some of the exit doors. It was necessary to fit strengthening beams below each door opening to stiffen up the structure.

Treacy soon made contact with the new lightweight units both in the Leeds area and in Cumbria. Perhaps the high front cab windows with sloping tops, and the destination blinds, reminded him of some of his ecclesiastical workplaces. Certainly the contrast with what had gone before touched a receptive chord, resulting in pictures featuring a diesel multiple unit in company with steam.

The diesel multiple unit was now set to take off. By late 1956 the Transport Commission could announce that 2401 vehicles had been ordered and over 270 were in service. Metropolitan Cammell was the largest private builder, but Cravens, Birmingham Railway Carriage & Wagon, Park Royal, Gloucester Carriage & Wagon, Wickham and Pressed Steel also added large numbers to the fleet. Within BR, Derby Works was busy producing railcars, now of steel construction. All were to a general specification of 150hp engines, fluid flywheels and epicyclic gearboxes, but each builder incorporated its own ideas on constructional methods, styling and other features. Various set sizes and combinations of power cars were catered for to suit the using area. Body layout variations began to abound, including suburban sets with

Portobello, east of Edinburgh with a Gloucester Railway Carriage & Wagon Co two-car dmu (to become class 100) heading for Rosewell & Hawthornden on the Peebles branch off the Waverley route c1958. The leading car is a driving motor brake composite in original livery. The main line was later slewed to ease the curves; the Craigentinny HST maintenance depot is now on land released to the left of the main line. All the steam locomotives in the yard are still of NBR origin, class N15s and J37s.

A class 104/1 four-car dmu built by the Birmingham Railway Carriage & Wagon Co in 1958 leaves York with a Sheffield train c1960. The train is in dmu livery of dark green with yellow whiskers on the front end and a white dome to the cab roof. It is lettered YK set which appears to be an allocation as this letter code was only officially introduced in 1973. The leading vehicle is driving motor composite No E50552.

An unusual Treacy Western Region photograph taken at Bristol Temple Meads station in 1971. The train is a Swindon cross country set introduced in 1957 becoming class 120. They are designed for the longer dmu services and had seating similar to the standard MkI vehicles. They have been replaced by Sprinters, unit No W50726 surviving until March 1987.

high density seating (which in this context meant multiple doors and precious little leg room) and parcels cars.

Swindon works concentrated on sets for the longer distance and intercity routes. The year 1957 saw new six car sets entering service on the Edinburgh Waverley–Glasgow Queen Street route; they comprised four power cars and two trailers, one of which provided buffet facilities. Despite their severe front end treatment, Treacy saw these as a suitable subject for his camera, though probably preferring the wraparound windscreens of the comparable sets, also with buffet cars, built by Swindon for Trans-Pennine running between Liverpool Lime Street and Leeds/Hull.

The Southern Region took a quite different line. With its electrification background it was not surprising that they should have preferred to use electric transmission. Their six car sets for the Hastings line had two power cars each containing a medium speed English Electric 500hp supercharged engine and dc generator in a compartment behind the driving cab; they entered service in 1957. Built to the restricted Hastings gauge they had a somewhat ungainly look about them; their performance on the steep grades through the Downs, with only 1000hp for 227 tons less provision for electric train heating, was to say the least pedestrian, and in the countryside they could be heard a couple of miles away. Nevertheless, lovingly maintained by the staff of St Leonards depot, Hastings, they proved highly reliable and long lived. The same general formula was used for suburban sets, in two and three coach formations, on the Central Division and in Hampshire.

Outside BR there was no shortage of informed 'experts' who considered that multiple units could never be economic on rural branch

The north end of Preston with two or more Craven two-car dmus leaving on an empty stock train for Blackpool Central c1960. The leading vehicle is a driving motor composite. This is one of the final batch of Craven dmus which were built with non standard engines and transmission. They were not a success and all were withdrawn before 1970.

A three-car suburban dmu built by Pressed Steel Co of Linwood being delivered to the Western Region. Leading car driving motor second W51385 heads the non-gangwayed dmu on the northern approaches to Shap in 1959 or 1960. The unit is in green livery with the moulded fibreglass cab roof/route indicator panel in white.

Paddington 1970. Brunel's original and cathedral like train shed of 1854 as seen by Eric Treacy's eyes in July 1970. Standing at platform 6 is a Pressed Steel Co suburban dmu made up of two three-car sets built to a 1959 Derby works design. The livery is blue with full yellow ends. The yellow bar is in evidence above the 1st class compartments as well as the figure 1 in place on the doors. The trailer composite also contained a lavatory and it was always advisable to use this vehicle on longer journeys as there were no gangways in the original design.

lines, and that something much less elaborate was needed, with branches reduced to something like light railway operation. In 1957 British Railways reacted to this pressure by ordering twenty-two four-wheeled railbuses, similar to the Uerdingen cars running widely in West Germany. Five firms, AC Cars, Bristol/Eastern Coachwork, Park Royal and Wickham from Britain, and Waggon und Maschinenbau from Germany, supplied different designs with horsepowers from 105 to 150. Only the German cars had conventional buffing and drawgear, but there was provision to tow the others in emergency. They pottered about branch lines from Wadebridge and East Anglia to Speyside; their seating capacity of about 50–55 was not always adequate, their reliability was not good and their riding qualities on branch line track was little better than that of the ACV sets. Almost all had been withdrawn by 1967, and Treacy seems never to have caught up with them.

At the opposite end of the spectrum, there was a market for deluxe high speed Pullman travel on a few intercity routes which could be met by self contained diesel trains, as had been proved with certain Trans-European Express services on the continent. A first class only service between Manchester Central and St Pancras in just over three hours was planned to relieve the West Coast route during electrification work, and business services between Bristol and Paddington in 110/115 minutes and between Wolverhampton/Birmingham and Paddington were projected. Five trains (two of six cars and three of eight cars) were ordered from Metropolitan Cammell in 1957 and came into service during 1960. A driving power car at each end contained a 1000hp MAN engine built by North British Locomotive under licence, with electric transmission involving fully suspended traction motors. Metro Cammell mounted them on Swiss Schlieren bogies built under licence. Air conditioning was provided, and maximum speed was 90mph. With their streamlined ends and eye catching livery of Nanking medium blue relieved by a broad white panel extending the length and depth of the window section in each car they were a joy to behold, and the interiors were to the high standards of true Pullman tradition; also in that tradition a supplementary fare was charged.

In service the Schlieren bogies very quickly proved the Achilles heel of the 'Blue Pullman' sets, for their riding qualities were, in a word, dreadful, and no maintenance or modification work was effective in getting them right. (BR's research into bogie design was barely under way at this time). There were unfortunate incidents during the serving of meals which prejudiced business confidence in them. With the electrification from Manchester Piccadilly to Euston in 1966, and the introduction of the new locomotive hauled 'Manchester Pullman' on that route, to a faster schedule with coaches on the excellent B4 and B5 bogies, all the diesel sets were concentrated on the Western Region. It was against the splendour of Brunel and Wyatt's Paddington station roof that Treacy chose to photograph them, and very fine they looked. But standards of passenger comfort had moved on since their inception, and they were withdrawn in 1973.

In late multiple unit builds there was scope for some change in the power equipment. The installation of 230hp Albion underfloor engines allowed the Marylebone services to be run with sets of two power cars and two trailers while still giving a power/weight ratio adequate for

126

Only five of these two-car units were ever made (in 1957) and of these a couple were withdrawn in 1961 and sold to the Trinidad Government Railway. Nevertheless they could be reckoned as being amongst the best of the second generation dmus – engines, riding and passenger comfort. However they had an integral body and frame structure making repairs expensive. The builders were D. Wickham & Co of Ware. The train in the photograph is entering Peterborough North station from the Great Eastern line c1963–4. The driving trailer composite No E56172 is complete with oil tail lamp.

A Birmingham Railway Carriage & Wagon Co three-car dmu heads away from Wakefield towards Hull over the L&Y main line c1963; the reporting number is incorrect. These units (for the North Eastern Region) were introduced in 1961 and later became class 110; they had Rolls Royce engines and incorporated a four character route indicator.

128

climbing the Chiltern Hills. The St Pancras–Bedford service was taken over by somewhat similar four car sets but equipped with 238hp Rolls-Royce engines driving through Twin Disc torque converters, and such sets also worked some Eastern Region services. The Rolls-Royce sets proved very troublesome, with cooling problems, engine seizures and transmission fires until the torque converter fluid was changed. Electrification to Bedford came only just in the nick of time; the delays in getting union agreement on one man operation of the electric Bed-Pan trains caused some very anxious moments indeed, and brought the diesel service to the brink of collapse.

Some of these multiple units had comparatively short lives, depending on their mechanical performance. The Craven-built cars, for instance, were troublesome and were withdrawn prematurely. The Metro-Cammell build, by contrast, soldiered on into the late 1980s, by which time their early attraction had given way to rattling windows, high noise levels and rather tatty internal panelling. Their rasping exhaust at high engine speeds remained until additional silencers were fitted from about 1980 onwards. Then, too, there were the cooling crises during heatwaves; overheated engines shut down and were assuaged with everything from watering cans to steam locomotive water cranes. In some areas drivers disliked having passengers watching

In 1960 a prestigious new dmu service was introduced between Liverpool, Manchester, Leeds and Hull. The Trans Pennine as it was named had new powerful multiple unit sets to cope with the sometimes severe gradients on the route. Originally built for six-car operation these were later reduced to five and four car units as can be seen with 1N22 heading through Heaton Lodge Junction in the mid 1960s. The centre car is a buffet first which proved to be uneconomic and was discontinued. Four of the cars in the original six coach sets had engines giving a total power output of 1840hp allowing much sharper timings than would have been possible with normal sets.

In 1960 a number of luxury Pullman diesel electric trains were introduced between Manchester Central–St Pancras, Paddington–Birmingham & Wolverhampton and Paddington–Bristol. One of the six-car all first Midland Pullman sets is seen here at St Pancras in its original blue and white livery. In order to gain maximum revenue from the sets they were run on a very intensive diagram, over the Midland route, southbound in the morning and return in the evening, coupled with a midday round trip to Nottingham. This gave a total of some 631 miles.

their every move and kept the cab blinds down, to the great annoyance of those behind; at the same time they often cut a small peephole in them in order to keep a voyeur's eye on what was happening in the saloon. Yet for some drivers the loneliness of command was an even worse fate, and cab doors were left open so that they could talk to interested passengers. The cabs were fascinating to watch; the peering at engine lights, the AWS noises, the despairing efforts of the guard playing on the heater control panel to mollify passengers who were frozen, baked alive or kippered by fumes from a perforated combustion heater. No such benefits and pleasures greet the passenger in today's Sprinters!

But they served their purpose and generated much new traffic for the railways, particularly in city and urban areas. On one Saturday morning in the late 1950s a two car dmu from Bacup and the Rossendale Valley disgorged no less than 230 passengers at Bury Bolton St – and that was just the ones not staying on to go to Manchester!

A Western Region eight Pullman car set standing alongside Paddington's platform 6 c1970. The set is made up of a motor brake 2nd, motor parlour car 1st, trailer kitchen 1st, trailer parlour car 1st (two), trailer kitchen 1st, motor parlour car 2nd and motor brake 2nd. The sets were built by Metro Cammell and were notoriously bad riders. They were withdrawn in 1973.

After the completion of the Euston–Manchester electrification in 1966 the Midland Pullmans were transferred to the Western Region and the sets were adapted for working in multiple. The LMR units were originally all 1st class the WR ones were not. Here two sets stand in Paddington c1970 painted in the later livery of grey, blue window surrounds and yellow nose. The train is made up to two of the six car Midland Pullman sets.

2 – Diesel Locomotives in the First Phase

If the diesel multiple unit element of the Modernisation Plan was broadly a success, albeit with some ragged edges, and the diesel shunting locomotive programme sailed along very serenely apart from two ventures into alternative engines, the main line diesel locomotive component proved to be a very mixed bag indeed. There were some successes by the standards of the time, but there were at least as many classes of very dubious value.

The British Transport Commission decided, very wisely, that in view of the potential problems and limited experience to date, 'softly, softly catchee monkey' should be the order of the day. There could be no question of the nationalised railway buying fully developed equipment from established overseas suppliers such as General Motors, and so it was necessary to rely on British diesel engine manufacturers.

For a variety of reasons the rail traction environment is particularly arduous for diesel engines. There was no standardised acceptance test to simulate operating conditions; today the UIC test procedure is extremely rigorous. With few exceptions, manufacturers' experience of this hard world had been limited at best to modest export orders; at worst it was nil. This thin lode would need to be worked on a broad face in the hope that, here and there, British Railways might strike gold; it was not going to be like buying a car. The experience of the previous seven years had demonstrated that the best approach would be to pitch them into a pattern of services worked from one or two depots; 'one offs' can give misleading information.

So it was planned to order about 170 diesel locomotives in three power ranges:-

Type A	600–800hp	40 locomotives
Type B	1000–1250hp	100 locomotives
Type C	2000hp	30 locomotives

The heavy emphasis at the low powered end was curious. Just what economic use could be made of a locomotive of only 600hp is difficult to appreciate. However, by the time the first orders were placed, late in 1955, the low powered group had moved upwards to 800–1000hp.

In the event, 174 locomotives of fourteen different classes were ordered, 141 of them to be built by six private firms, and the remainder in BR workshops for which the engines and transmission equipment were ordered separately. Diesel engines came from seven manufacturers and electric transmission equipment from six. Eight of the locomotives, for use on the Western Region were to use hydraulic rather than electric transmission, with two different systems being evaluated. The smallest single order was for three locomotives (quickly supplemented by further orders), the largest for twenty. It is not clear now how far the initiative for hydraulic transmissions came from Paddington and Swindon, but probably Riddles at the Railway Executive smiled wryly at the prospect of the Western Region being different from the rest!

Through 1956 the policy on pilot orders was maintained. In

A contrast of motive power at Leeds Holbeck c1962–3. On the left is the new fuelling point with three Peak class locomotives, note the variations in headcode panels and gangway doors. The two diesels in the background look distinctly odd as the buffers and drawgear are on the bogies Hornby train fashion – a legacy from O.V. Bulleid/English Electric Holbeck's steam round-house entrances are in the background with a Black 5 behind D14.

Berwick upon Tweed Royal Border bridge westside from the north bank looking to Tweedmouth and Spittal. A down cement train hauled by a class 40 is crossing the bridge in the late 1960s. The train is composed entirely of 'Presflo' wagons.

The Cliffe–Uddingston cement tanks pass through York station hauled by class 33 No D6576 c1964. This was a very long through locomotive working and one which brought class 33s off their native heath and, depending on the route through London, over the metals of three and possibly five other regions. D6576 was an early casualty being withdrawn from service in November 1968 after accident damage.

8 April 1989 at York. Looking south from the station footbridge much has changed, the two middle roads have been lifted and the catenary erected. In the bay platforms a new generation of diesel multiple units is in evidence. From 11 May 1989 the platforms were renumbered, No 8a on the left is now No 3 and No 9a and b on the right No 5. (John Edgington)

135

November the Commission said that until thorough and selective trials have been completed "the Commission intends to restrict further orders to comparatively small numbers."

But this procurement policy now changed fundamentally. Early in 1957 repeat orders were placed for forty seven locomotives, before any of the original orders had been delivered. Late that year, three further orders for 156 locomotives were placed, again before delivery had started. The first locomotive against the original orders (class 20) was delivered in June 1957.

Also in late 1957 came a revision of the preliminary three band power classification in favour of a five band type listing to match subsequent orders, which lasted until the class number system was introduced in 1968:-

Type	1	750–1000hp
	2	1000–1250hp
	3	1500–1750hp
	4	2000–2500hp
	5	3000hp upwards

A favourite location for many photographers, Edinburgh Princes Street gardens, with The Mound tunnel and the National Gallery in the background. Two Sulzer powered type 2 Bo-Bo diesel electrics (later class 26) head a down express for Aberdeen on the north roads. This is a 1959/60 picture.

Had the BTC stuck to its original (and thoroughly laudable) policy, there would have been a lengthy interregnum while the fourteen designs were evaluated in service, before placing further orders. But BR could not afford such a delay; they wanted a steady changeover from steam to diesel traction, and the builders were looking for continuity of work. Preliminary judgements had to be made, and this would involve a strong element of risk. The initial orders perhaps reflected that risk assessment; of the fourteen classes, initial orders for nine were for ten locomotives or less.

No further orders were placed for four classes (16, 23, 28 and 41), none of which lasted more than twelve years after delivery of the last example. Four further classes (15, 21, 22 and 42/43) were reordered in modest numbers, only to suffer a similar early fate. This left six classes (or uprated derivations) which were reordered in very substantial numbers and which emerged as potentially sound, reliable locomotives with lives of twenty years or more. They were the English Electric class 20, the BR-built, classes 24 and 25, the comparable Birmingham RC&W classes 26 and 27, the Brush class 31 – though they needed to be re-engined to earn their place in the fleet – the English Electric class 40 and the BR-built family of classes 44, 45 and 46. To these must be added the Birmingham RC&W class 33, which is only now coming to the end of its life.

Of the original Type 1 designs, only the English Electric class 20 has stood the test of time and is still in arduous use on merry-go-round and other block trains. For this work many are fitted with slow speed

In 1957 the Vulcan Foundry began building Type 1 1000hp diesel electric locomotives, now class 20. These were given trial runs from Newton-le-Willows to Penrith via Edge Hill and back before being put into traffic. No D8002 is seen heading through Carnforth with eight empty coaches on 16 July 1957. The station is visible in the background with the Furness and Furness & Midland Joint lines platforms curving away sharply to the left.

137

Penrith with class 20 No D8037 arriving in September or October 1959. The Cockermouth Keswick & Penrith line diverges behind the train and the small locomotive depot can just be seen at the right hand side of the picture. (The coach is a Stanier corridor brake third and modellers may note the grey painted panels on the double doors and the two types of ventilators on the coach roof).

Class 20 No D8106 heads a fitted freight out of Dumfries yard in August 1971. The site of the steam locomotive shed is on the left with the ramp of the coaling stage still prominent. Treacy used the road bridges at each end of Dumfries station as vantage points.

Eric Treacy's only photograph of an NBL/MAN class 21 taken as it emerges from the suburban platforms at Edinburgh Waverley station in the mid 1960s. Originally No D6116 was stationed at Stratford (30A) but was soon transferred to Scotland. Note the reuse of the old lattice post for the colour light signal and that someone may have been playing the fool – the headcode is for the Royal Train.

Ten of the type B or 2 locomotives were ordered from English Electric under the Modernisation Plan; they used a single Napier Deltic engine and all were delivered in 1959. These class 23 Bo-Bos proved heavy on maintenance and were later rebuilt at the Vulcan Foundry (1963–65). Eric Treacy found this unidentified member of the class, in its original condition between Gas Works and Copenhagen tunnels c1960.

Baby Deltic class 23 No D5901 (with refurbished engine and four character route indicator) heads a Kings Cross–Cambridge Buffet Car express approaching Potters Bar c1965. The buffet service in this train is still provided by one of the long lived Gresley designs, the rest of the train being made up of MkI vehicles. The Cambridge Buffet Expresses were introduced by the LNER in 1932 (and nicknamed the Beer Trains) using the GNR main line rather than the GER route. The facility lasted until 1978 when the Kings Cross–Royston electric service commenced.

control and are operated in multiple with cabs outwards to qualify for single manning. Looking back it is interesting to note that production was discontinued after 128 had been built, in favour of the Clayton class 17s; when these proved most unsatisfactory, production of class 20s was resumed in 1966. The Paxman engine in classes 15 and 16 proved troublesome, even on the less-than-arduous cross-London freight traffic, and they were withdrawn by 1971 and 1968 respectively, apparently unrecorded by Treacy in their suburban haunts.

The ten Type 2 classes fared a little better, but not much. The MAN engine built by North British Locomotive under license for classes 21 and 22 was a maintenance nightmare, though marginally less so with hydraulic transmission in the 22s than in the diesel-electric 21s. The class 29s derived from class 21s and using the Paxman engine was better but far from perfect and did not warrant retention beyond 1971, three years longer than the 21s. The Baby Deltics (class 23) used a highly rated version of the Deltic engine which did not take kindly to the power cycle of inner and outer suburban work from Kings Cross, and were all withdrawn by 1971. The Met-Vick Crossley class 28s, with their highly unusual Co-Bo arrangement dictated by heavy-weight construction, quickly proved an engine maintenance headache, as might have been anticipated from their cousins running on CIE. They were soon put into store pending refurbishment by the builders;

140

Class 24 Bo-Bo No D5079 on the last stretch to Ais Gill summit with a down stopping train of one hundred per cent LMS stock – the leading coach is a corridor brake third which could well date back to 1926, followed by Stanier designs. No D5079 had a life of only sixteen years entering service in February 1960 and withdrawn in July 1976; the photograph is dated between October 1960 and May 1961 when it was on loan to Carlisle Upperby shed.

A location well away from Treacy's usual haunts, Tywyn Gwynedd in September 1971. Class 24 No 5143 heads the daily pick up freight from Pwllheli (if required) or Penrhyndeudraeth. The staple traffic was explosives from Cookes factory at Penrhyndeudraeth and there are five gunpowder vans in the consist. The train is signalled into the shunting neck extension no doubt prior to shunting in Tywyn yard.

Going north from Inverness. Class 24 Bo-Bo No 5124 leaves the old Highland Railway's terminus for Wick and Thurso (via Georgemas Junction) around 1969–70. The signal post on the left is pure Highland Railway but fitted with an LMS upper quadrant semaphore.

A well known location in typical Settle–Carlisle weather c1970. Class 25 No 5190 heads the up pick-up freight at Ais Gill and looks as if it is about to be shunted into the up refuge siding for an up express. Although the station goods yards along the line were nearly all closed by this date private sidings were still open for this pick-up service.

An unidentifiable class 26 Bo-Bo enters Achnasheen station with a train from Inverness around 1962–3. The locomotive is fitted with tablet exchange apparatus for use on the Highland main line – this did not exist on the Kyle road. Note the tablet ready for collection. The make up of the train is an interesting one, behind the refrigerator van are six Stanier design coaches though at least one was a BR built product. Bringing up the rear is the Devon Belle observation car which was rebuilt from a third class Pullman.

Class 26 No D5344 leads class 24 D5118 past the Lochgorm works of the old Highland Railway in the very late 1960s or even 1970. No 5344 spent most of its working life at Inverness but was withdrawn in 1984 after damage whilst clearing snow. The third coach is a griddle car, built at Wolverton in 1961 and carried on Commonwealth type bogies. Only seven of these vehicles were made and No 1100 is now preserved at the NRM.

The south end of Perth station with two class 26 locomotives on an Inverness–Glasgow express c1972. The leading engine is No 5331 carrying an odd livery of blue with numbers at both ends of the body and the logo on the right hand cab. The left hand cab has provision for tablet exchange apparatus but this is not fitted no doubt because the Highland line was then signalled by tokenless block. The second locomotive has the more usual arrangement of number only on the right hand cab and cannot be identified. A Metro Cammell dmu stands in the right hand platform and a TPO in the North British bay.

143

Class 27s at Fort William. Double headed Nos 5362 and 5349 leave the old station with a restaurant car train for Glasgow Queen Street in April 1970. The leading engine is repainted in blue with full yellow ends but the second is still in its original Brunswick green. The class was built at BRCW's Smethwick works, now closed.

Quad-Art suburban. One of the later batches of Brush type 2 diesel electrics, A1A–A1A (later class 31) No D5603 heads out of Kings Cross with a down local. The photograph was taken from Copenhagen Junction signal box, a familiar Eric Treacy location. In the background is one of the unhappy Thompson L1 class 2-6-4 tanks with two gangwayed full brakes of LMS and MkI design. The photograph was taken around 1960–1 and by then most of the L1 tanks had been replaced, with the suburban services run by diesels or dmus.

The Uddingston–Cliffe cement
empties approaching York hauled by
class 33 No D6576. This was
probably a regular locomotive for
the turn (see pages 135, 159). The
location of this photograph is
difficult to make out but residents of
York will recognise Poppleton Road
school above the middle of the train.

A very early photograph of a class
40 No D235 (named Apapa in
1962) pulling out of Euston in 1960
at the head of a Liverpool express.
The locomotive is dark green with
light green band and no yellow
warning panel on the nose.
Over in platform 1 is a class 24 on
empty stock (in spite of express
passenger headcode). Loaded trains
did not usually leave from this
platform prior to the rebuilding of
the station.

One of the LMR English Electric
type 4 1Co-Co1 locomotives (the
initial pilot scheme batch had gone
to the Eastern Region) D211 leaves
Carlisle with a Perth to Euston train
in 1959 or 1960. It received the
name Mauretania at Liverpool
Riverside station in September 1960.
The leading coaches are of LMS
design, the brake third may be BR
built whilst the second appears to be
a steel panelled vestibule. An early
Derby 'Lightweight' dmu stands in
the Maryport and Carlisle bay. The
yard pilot is still a 'Jinty' 0-6-0 tank.

thereafter for a while they ran the fast overnight Condor container service between Hendon and Glasgow – hardly suitable for Treacy's photographic style – but were withdrawn after a life which in some cases did not reach ten years.

The only satisfactory machines in this Type were those of classes 24 and 26, the uprated classes 25 and 27, and the class 31 after re-engining. Treacy seemed to take most interest in the Bo-Bos working in Scotland, from Edinburgh to the remote Highlands, often in multiple. He does not appear to have encountered the twenty class 27s modified for push-pull working (one at each end of the train, electronically multipled through the coach lighting jumpers) on the fast Edinburgh–Glasgow service, on which they were replaced by class 47/7s after eight years of gruelling work. The class 31s, most of which are still with us, looked at one time likely to have the short life of many other classes; they were closely based on locomotives built for Sri Lanka in 1953, using the Mirrlees engine. Within six years this engine was in serious trouble, but its replacement by an English Electric engine gave the locomotive a new lease of life.

The Type 3 category was represented in this phase only by the class 33, which was in essence a class 27 with larger engine providing electric train heating to meet Southern Region needs. The control gear is notable in providing for multipling with EMUs. Among the jobs that often took them far from their home territory Treacy came across them at York on the Cliffe–Uddingston bulk cement trains. They also came to prominence on the push-pull workings between Bournemouth and Weymouth prior to electrification.

No less than seven classes fell within Type 4, ranging from the extremely heavy (in relation to their power) classes 40, 44, 45 and 46, using the four axle bogies pioneered by the three Southern prototypes, to the lightweight B-B class 42 and 43 diesel hydraulics on only four axles. The class 40s (whistlers to the railfans, thanks to the sibilant sound of their turbochargers) proved one of the most dependable designs, though underpowered, and lasted until 1985; a feature of interest in their youth – and one which Treacy did not fail to capture – was the waterscoop for replenishing the heating boiler tank from track troughs. The locomotive could almost disappear in a cloud of spray when used, which was fine for photographers but unkind to electrical equipment. The comparable classes 44, 45 and 46 with Sulzer power also proved generally sound, and the greater power enabled some class 45s to be modified to provide electric train heating, thus prolonging their life until 1988. One class 46 came to a spectacular end in 1984 when it hit a nuclear flask at 90mph at Old Dalby as part of a proving test – for the flask! Treacy photographed them on all sorts of work, no more than on his much-loved Settle & Carlisle line.

Of the three diesel hydraulic classes, it could be argued that the pairing of engines and transmissions was unfortunate. The five locomotives of class 41 and the thirty-three of class 43 had MAN/North British engines, which needed heavy and continuous maintenance, but splendid Voith transmissions. They lasted no more than ten years. By contrast the class 42 had excellent Maybach engines but the less suitable Mekydro transmissions. They lasted a little longer than the other two classes, but official policy had no role for diesel hydraulics and even the 42s had gone by 1972.

146

The west end of Edinburgh Waverley station c1969 with class 40 No D263 standing in platform 15 on a northbound express. The loco is still in green livery but has acquired a full yellow nose. It was one of seven locomotives built with disc codes but rebuilt at Haymarket depot with a square cornered four character route indicator box. Although withdrawn in 1984 No 40063 received the name Express Link and was used as an exhibition locomotive; it was subsequently scrapped in 1987. To the right is a Swindon built InterCity dmu in blue and grey livery on a Glasgow express.

Saturday 1 May 1976 saw the centenary of the opening to passengers of the Settle–Carlisle route. This was marked in style by the running of three special trains including one for invited guests from Carnforth. This had been steam hauled by two preserved locomotives, LNER A3 No 4472 Flying Scotsman and LNWR Precedent class 2-4-0 No 790 Hardwicke as far as Hellifield. The remainder of the journey was behind diesel electric No 40083 seen at Carlisle with the train of historic coaches.

Class 44 No D2 Helvellyn ascending Shap at the head of a train of empty carriages c1960. Apart from a few forays over the southern end of the West Coast main line and on the Midland c1959–60 the class 44s did not regularly work passenger trains.

The down Waverley. Peak class 45 1Co-Co1 No D20 heads 1S64 past Wortley Junction signalbox on the Midland main line in the summer of 1961 or 1962. The stock is in maroon livery and all MkI except for the fifth vehicle, an LMS twelve wheeled dining car. The rear of the train is passing the site of Holbeck Low Level station closed in 1958.

The north portal of Blea Moor tunnel with the up Waverley hauled by a class 45 approaching c1964. The leading coach MkI M35339 is a corridor brake second. Note the placing of the distant signal giving a clear view from the tunnel. There are still signs of the construction of the line around the tunnel mouth with mounds of spoil and what appears to be the course of an incline running up the hillside.

1M86 at Dumfries. The up Thames–Clyde express passes the shed on a very dull day around 1967 or 1968; it is headed by Peak class 45 No D13. Sitting outside the shed is class 27 No D5350 with one of its bogies out and thirty ton crane RS 1071 is in attendance. The engine has a blackened area round the No 1 end so there has possibly been a traction motor fire. Ironically the attendant engine, class 20 D8109 was itself withdrawn after accident damage in 1982.

Class 46 1Co-Co1 No D177 passing Copley Hill shed, on the GNR main line out of Leeds, at the head of the up Yorkshire Pullman c1963. The train is made up of six Metro-Cammell Pullman coaches with a 1928 brake at the rear.

Up White Rose. The 15.09 Bradford Exchange (15.30 Leeds Central) to Kings Cross leaves Peascliffe tunnel north of Grantham behind class 46 No D189 of Leeds Holbeck (55A) in the late summer of 1963. The stock is all BR Mk1 and the roofboard reads Kings Cross–Leeds. The Leeds and Bradford portions ran separately to Wakefield and were joined there.

The down Thames–Clyde express leaves Dumfries for Glasgow Central in August 1971 – the original northern terminus of the train, the GSWR St Enoch, having closed in 1966. The locomotive is class 46 No 193 the final member of the class to be delivered – in January 1963. This kind of cross country express working was typical of the duties performed by the class until their demise in 1984.

PRODUCTION
FIRST PHASE DIESEL LOCOMOTIVES

BR Class	Year Introduced	Builder	Wheel Arrangement	Engine Horsepower	Engine	Transmission	Max. Speed	No. Built	Original BR Numbers
15*	1957	Yorkshire Engine Co (10) and Clayton Equipment (34)	Bo-Bo	800	Paxman 16YHXL	BTH electric	60	44	D8200–8243
16*	1958	North British Loco	Bo-Bo	800	Paxman 16YHXL	GEC electric	60	10	D8400–8409
20*	1957	English Electric/ Vulcan Foundry and R. Stephenson, Hawthorn	Bo-Bo	1000	English Electric 8SVT Mk II	EE electric	75 (Note 1)	228	D8000–8199 D8300–8327
21*	1958	North British Loco	Bo-Bo	1100 (Note 2)	MAN/NBL L12V18/21	EE electric	75	58	D6100–6157
22*	1959	North British Loco	B-B	1000 / 1100	MAN/NBL L12V18/21A (7 locomotives) L12V18/21B (remainder)	Voith/NBL hydraulic	75	58	D6300–6357
23*	1959	English Electric/Vulcan Foundry	Bo-Bo	1100	Napier Deltic T9–29	EE electric	75	10	D5900–5909
24*	1958	BR Derby, Crewe and Darlington	Bo-Bo	1160	Sulzer 6LDA28A	BTH electric	75	151	D5000–5150
25*	1961	BR Darlington and Derby Beyer Peacock	Bo-Bo	1250	Sulzer 6LDA28B	AEI electric	90	323	D5151–5299 D7500–7677
26*	1958	Birmingham RC&W	Bo-Bo	1160	Sulzer 6LDA28A	Crompton Parkinson electric	75	47	D5300–5346
27*	1961	Birmingham RC&W	Bo-Bo	1250	Sulzer 6LDA28B	GEC electric	90	69	D5347–5415
28*	1958	Metropolitan Vickers	Co-Bo	1200	Crossley HSTV8	MV electric	75	20	D5700–5719
29	1965	Rebuilt by BR St. Rollox from class 21	Bo-Bo	1350	Paxman 12YJXL	EE electric	80	20	Between D6100 and D6137
31*	1957	Brush	A1A-A1A	1250 (Note 3)	Mirrlees JVS12T (Note 3)	Brush electric	75 80 90 (Note 3)	263	D5500–5699 D5800–5862
33	1960	Birmingham RC&W	Bo-Bo	1550	Sulzer 8LDA28B	Crompton Parkinson electric	85	98	D6500–6597
40*	1958	English Electric/ Vulcan and R. Stephenson, Hawthorn	1-Co-Co-1	2000	English Electric 16SVT Mk II	EE electric	90	200	D200–399
41*	1958	North British Loco	A1A-A1A	2000	(2) MAN/NBL L12V18/21A	(2) Voith L306r hydraulic	90	5	D600–604
42*	1958	BR Swindon	B-B	2000 (Note 4)	(2) Maybach MD650 (Note 4)	(2) Mekydro K104 hydraulic	90	38	D800–832 D866–870
43*	1960	North British Loco	B-B	2200	(2) MAN/NBL L12V18/21B	(2) Voith L306r hydraulic	90	32	D833–865
44*	1959	BR Derby	1-Co-Co-1	2300	Sulzer 12LDA28A	Crompton Parkinson electric	90	10	D1–10
45	1960	BR Derby and Crewe	1-Co-Co-1	2500	Sulzer 12LDA28B	Crompton Parkinson electric	90	127	D11–137
46	1961	BR Derby	1-Co-Co-1	2500	Sulzer 12LDA28B	Brush electric	90	56	D138–193

Notes: 1 Maximum speed reduced to 60mph in 1987.
2 Horsepower later reduced to 1000 to improve reliability.
3 After first twenty locomotives the Mirrlees engine was uprated to 1365hp. From 1964 all locomotives rebuilt with English Electric 12SVT engine rated at 1470hp. D5520–5535 geared for 80mph maximum, D5536 on for 90mph.
4 D804–829, D831–2, D866–870 rated at 2200hp, D830 at 2400hp with Paxman 12YJXL engines.
* Included in initial orders.

152

3 – Later Phases – Diesel Locomotives

The locomotives ordered in phase one formed a curiously unbalanced fleet. There were a mere 161 type 1 machines, but type 2 had been greatly over subscribed and exceeded 1200 locomotives. The type 3 concept was represented only by the 98 class 33s. The highest horsepower group, in type 4, could only muster 469 locomotives, of which only 183 could provide as much as 2500hp. The fleet was failing to keep up with the operators' hopes for faster passenger trains and heavier and faster freight trains. Even on secondary services the numerous locomotives in type 2 could not produce the performance sought. These were the Beeching years.

Thus, between mid-1959 and 1961, following the first learning phase, and even though further locomotives in the lower power ranges were being ordered, those for *new* classes were with one exception concentrated on type 3 (about 1750hp) and type 4 (about 2700hp) locomotives. Seven new classes were built – see table on page 166 – two diesel hydraulics and five diesel electrics, and these continued in production until 1965. One new manufacturer, Beyer Peacock, was brought into the fold. Cast steel bogies and integral body construction were adopted exclusively, and with the exception of the class 37 and the Deltic, noses were *out*. Only the Clayton class 17 proved to be short-lived, and the classes 37 and 47 were still going strongly after twenty-five years.

Portobello East Junction in the mid 1960s with class 17 No D8571 on an up freight ostensibly bound for the Eastern Region (9E46) although it is an Edinburgh district local trip freight; the first seven wagons are sheeted, they probably contain esparto grass (for paper making) from Granton Harbour and are headed for Millerhill yard. This class of locomotive enjoyed a very short life, No D8571 lasted from January 1964 to May 1969.

The class 17 was intended to replace the class 20, but its performance proved disastrously unreliable and led instead to further orders for the latter. The central cab was over 12ft long and became very hot in summer; men said that it was big enough to hold a dance in. All were in due course banished to Scotland, where Treacy made their acquaintance on Edinburgh area freight trip work. The abiding memory of their brief lives is of twin clouds of black smoke belching from their exhaust pipes. By 1971 all had been withdrawn.

The two diesel hydraulics, classes 35 (Hymek) and 52 (Western) proved quite good overall performers. The Hymek finally overcame the objection to its forerunners of needing 'two of everything' to get the desired power. The Western was based on drawings of a German demonstrator locomotive and its front end treatment was distinctive. It suffered some early problems with rough riding and vibration, but after their cure it settled down to some excellent work. But diesel hydraulics were doomed under BR's future traction policy, and the impending closure of Swindon works was only the last straw. All had gone by 1977, but these last two classes were undoubtedly the best. Treacy saw quite a lot of them on his visits to Paddington and seemed to find a certain affinity with the 52s in particular.

The diesel electric classes (the Deltics of class 55 are dealt with in the next chapter) proved to be the most successful of all the second phase locomotives, and are likely to remain in service for another decade. Both the class 37 and the class 47 (the latter after derating) have proved real workhorses on a full range of duties, though the 47

Class 35 B-B No 7039 at Temple Meads station during the construction of the GPO access bridge. By the time Treacy was able to photograph the WR diesel hydraulics all had been painted in 'corporate image' rail blue. No 7039 has the raised letter D painted over (the prefix being dropped when the conflict with steam locomotive numbers no longer applied after 1968) whilst the figures are also in metal. The body styling of the class was unlike the other Western Region hydraulics being more akin to the Brush types. Withdrawal began in 1971 as the class was by then considered to be non standard.

is not entirely happy on heavy, slow speed slogging. Five built with a vee-formation version of the Sulzer engine were, however, much less satisfactory and soon reverted to standard. Both classes have been adapted for specific haulage roles under BR's sector organisation.

Prominent in Treacy's pictures of all these classes was the four digit headcode on the locomotive identifying the class of train, its destination area and serial number. It was displayed to help signalmen and others in the identification and regulation of trains, but with the spread of power signal boxes with automatic train description on the signalling panel it proved superfluous and was abolished in the 1970s.

Once the orders for these seven classes were well under way or complete, there was a pause while they were evaluated and (perhaps more important) while the users struggled to decide what they would need in the future. In the freight field the wagon load business was declining in favour of block Freightliner and bulk haul trains for oil, coal and minerals. The ever-growing emphasis was on higher power. The class 47 was handling this traffic, but its limitations in low speed power and adhesion were being reached. On the passenger side the 1960s saw the general change from steam to electric train heating initiated in order to improve reliability, facilitate air conditioning and eliminate the need for a second man to tend the boiler. This needed a separate heating generator, engine driven, which ate into the power available for traction. It was not an option which could be readily applied to diesel hydraulic locomotives.

It was this electric heating requirement that spawned the class 50 design in English Electric minds. Before electrification of the West Coast route through to Glasgow (not completed until 1974) the

South of Finsbury Park with the up Master Cutler Pullman (Sheffield–Kings Cross) hauled by class 37 No D6813. The first train taking this name was introduced in 1947 running via the Great Central route between Marylebone and Sheffield Victoria. In 1958 this became a Pullman service and was rerouted over the Great Northern main line from Kings Cross. The title was dropped in 1968 but subsequently revived for a London Midland Region express between St Pancras and Sheffield Midland.

155

York in the mid 1960s. English Electric type 3 Co-Co No D6771 approaches Holgate Bridge Junction. The locomotive was one of sixty seven built by Robert Stephenson & Hawthorns the majority coming from the Vulcan Foundry. The train of RSJs and plate steel will have come from Teeside as the reporting number 7E16 is the 13.40 Tees yard–Whitemoor. The open ground to the left of the locomotive was once the site of the roundhouses making up York South shed.

York Easter 1989. The view from Holgate bridge whilst track alterations were in progress. The main lines have since been laid on the new ballast to the right. The Leeds lines and the goods lines have been relaid and electrification masts erected. In the background a class 47 in Railfreight's Petroleum Sector livery waits at the head of a tanker train. (John Edgington)

English Electric class 37 No D6817 runs through Wakefield Kirkgate's centre roads at the head of a class 6 – partially fitted – freight c1966. Note the SNCF ferry vans 4th–10th vehicles. These medium powered locomotives (1750hp) proved to be extremely successful and many have recently been refurbished to prolong their lives into the 1990s.

A section of railway which has now disappeared. The East Coast main line just south of Chaloners Whin Junction, York which was superseded by the Selby diversion in 1983 to avoid subsidence from the new coalfield. Class 37 No D6803 heads 1E46 south in the mid 1960s.

Peterborough North. The station, in a somewhat dilapidated state, looking north towards Doncaster and York sometime in the mid 1960s. The train, reporting No 1B30 an up Cleethorpes–Kings Cross service, is hauled by one of the earlier English Electric class 37s or type 3s as they were known. The loco has gangway doors and split headcode boxes, it is in green livery with a small yellow warning panel and dates from 1962. This is an historic scene as the station is now rebuilt and the ECML electrified. The old Great Northern Hotel stood to the right of the photograph. There appears to be a crew change here. Note the old steam uniform with greasetop caps.

coaching stock had been dual heated to allow diesel locomotives with steam boilers to work Anglo-Scottish trains north of Crewe. The 50s (Hoovers to their fans) developed from the highly successful DP2 prototype and provided electric heat from the start. At first they were leased by BR from English Electric, not being purchased until 1974. They proved immensely troublesome; despite their DP2 ancestry the complications built into them to fit them for almost every job on the railway seriously affected their reliability. Treacy probably knew little of this, no doubt being more impressed by the fact that when working in multiple on the Royal Scot they went up Shap at such speed that it was necessary to reduce power to observe the 60mph restriction then in force at the summit! Their continued problems when transferred to the Western Region led to a heavy refurbishment programme which included a ruthless comb-out of unnecessary features and some updating of their electronics, but this has been only partially successful; they should be with us well into the decade. This spread of electric train heating was also catered for by retrospectively fitting main engine-

A total of 512 Brush type 4s was built between 1962 and 1967. The original member of the class (47) No D1500 heads south through Doncaster with a cement empties train bound for Cliffe on the Southern Region. The first batch of twenty locomotives were built with electric as well as steam train heating equipment although this was not standard as a batch was constructed with no train heating at all. This photograph is one of the few accurately dated by Eric Treacy, 31 July 1963.

Lofthouse colliery between Wakefield and Ardsley provides the background for this Treacy picture. Class 47 No D1510 heads a southbound express 1E15 on a fine summer evening in the mid 1960s. The stock is mostly Mk1 in maroon livery, but the third vehicle is a new Mk2 corridor first carried on B4 bogies. The line running off to the right in front of the colliery is part of the Methley Joint line (owned by the GN, L&Y and NE Railway Companies), one of the many joint lines in this mining area.

Another unusually murky picture for Eric Treacy but one full of interest. Brush type 4 Co-Co No D1519 rounds the curve at Geldard Junction – for Leeds Central – c1965. In the summer of 1964 the Queen of Scots Pullman had been discontinued as such and this service from Kings Cross to Harrogate (via Leeds where a Bradford portion was detached) took the name The White Rose. The old NER (originally Leeds Northern Railway) roundhouse is in the background – today it is still in use as a garage.

Wakefield Kirkgate the former
Lancashire & Yorkshire Railway
station on the Calder Valley line in
the mid 1960s. Class 47 No D1511
heads a Kings Cross–Leeds service.
The station has now fallen on hard
times, is unstaffed and is served by
an hourly Leeds, Castleford,
Wakefield, Barnsley and Sheffield
service plus an irregular Wakefield
Westgate–Huddersfield service.

Down mineral train. Class 47 No
D1516 passes the fine old GNR
signal box at Crescent Junction
Peterborough sometime in the mid
1960s. Note the steam engine type
Finsbury Park (34G) shed plate
below the indicator box.

Class 47 No D1513 heads 4S35, the 11.00 Kings Cross–Aberdeen towards St James' Bridge Doncaster in the summer of 1965. This fast fitted freight, due Doncaster at 15.47, conveyed empty meat containers and fish vans; the first seventeen wagons are conflats. To the right with the stock for 2N57, a Doncaster–Leeds service, is an unknown class 31.

Class 47 diesel electric No D1831 in two tone green with a full yellow front heads an up company freightliner reporting No 4M41 from Linwood near Paisley to Gosford Green descending from Shap summit sometime in the late 1960s. The containers conveyed parts for Rootes car plants.

driven heating generators to numbers of locomotives in classes 31, 37, 45 and 47, producing new numbers and sub-classes.

No new locomotive class now appeared for nine years. The passenger workload could be covered, despite the withdrawal of less satisfactory designs, by the creeping spread of electrification, the introduction of High Speed Trains, and more intensive fleet utilisation. But hard economics was demanding heavier freight train loads and locomotives capable of working them single handed over the pinchpoints of the system. This resulted in four new heavy freight-dedicated locomotive classes, only one of which appeared just before Treacy's unexpected death in 1978 and which, so far as we know, he never saw in the flesh.

The class 56 was from the same Brush stable as the class 47, and in many respects it derived from that design but with a Ruston Paxman (née English Electric) engine instead of the heavy Sulzer unit. The first thirty were built – very poorly – by subcontract in Romania because at the time Brush was hard-pressed by other orders. They have now been the standard power for merry-go-round coal trains for a decade in some areas, notably based at Knottingley to serve the Aire Valley power stations. The class 58 was an attempt to build a comparable locomotive in simpler form, with better maintenance accessibility and with export potential. It also pioneered a new and successful cab

Amazon at Dumfries. Western Region class 47 Co-Co No 1675 (named in November 1965) takes the southbound 14.50 Glasgow–Liverpool express through Dumfries station in August 1971. The fine GSWR canopies are still extant and compare well with the somewhat sober station buildings.

layout. All fifty are allocated to Toton depot. In both cases maximum load has been limited by adhesion deficiencies; colliery sidings in particular are notorious for bad rail conditions.

Much research into this problem, on both sides of the Atlantic, has centred on separate field excitation of dc traction motors (Sepex) and the associated control gear to provide for strictly regulated wheelslip. In the USA this has been successfully developed and proven by General Motors as the Super Series Wheel Creep Control to maximise drawbar pull for any given railhead condition. The class 59, bought from GM and owned not by BR but by Foster Yeoman Ltd, incorporates the Super Series system and has demonstrated how this enables it to lift loads appreciably greater than is possible for a 56 or 58. Rival quarry owners ARC have now also ordered similar machines from GM. The class 60 has, at the time of writing, only recently appeared and has yet to prove that its Brush Sepex system can match the American product.

How Treacy would surely have relished the class 59, its front end, its body with high floor level and distinctive livery of silver and grey with light blue stripes, and with a long train of bogie limestone hoppers in tow, in some cases grossing over four thousand tons. He might even have been tempted to bend his rule of not using his camera under winter lighting conditions!

Class 50 No D441 plus an unidentifiable member of the class passing the remains of Kingmoor shed (buildings intact but track removed) c1970. The train is the down Royal Scot and with double headed class 50s it could really move – climbing Shap at 80 mph was still very much an experience then.

English Electric class 50 No D401, *later* Dreadnought *crosses the river Eden at Etterby north of Carlisle with 1S55 the 11.00 Motorail service from Kensington Olympia to Perth in August 1970. All fifty members of the class were built in* fourteen months but were not originally sold to BR, only leased. A plate on the body side reads 'This locomotive is the property of English Electric Leasings Limited'; they were removed on purchase. Eric Treacy photographed the class when first introduced on the Anglo-Scottish services; they later replaced the hydraulics on the Western Region and are probably No 1 in many diesel enthusiasts' affections today.

Paddington arrival. Now preserved on the Severn Valley Railway class 52 No D1013 Western Ranger *has just come to a halt at platform 8 with 1A65 the 15.55 ex Paignton and passengers are scurrying for the taxi rank; the date (check with the lady's skirt) is 1970. Although they survived until 1977 the Westerns never received a new TOPS number and therefore retained their (GWR steam type) cast number plates until the end. The engine's allocation number (87A Swansea Landore) has been painted just behind the cab door. Below the number plate is a panel giving the class details.*

One of the diesel enthusiasts' favourite classes; No D1061 Western Envoy waits at Paddington with 1F60 a down express (probably for South Wales as the engine was allocated to Landore shed, Swansea) in the summer of 1970. The Westerns, later class 52s, originally emerged from Swindon works in 1961 though a number were built at Crewe, including D1061 in April 1963. In the adjacent platform is class 47 No 1678 (an Old Oak Common engine) still in two tone green livery but now with full yellow ends and cab window surround.

Class 52 No D1010 Western Campaigner with a long unidentified express made up of MkI and MkII stock approaches Paddington in 1970. Many of the MkIs as well as MkIIs are carried on 1963 Swindon designed B4 bogies which gave a much improved ride over the original MkI bogies. No D1010 was withdrawn in 1977, one of the last to go. It was purchased for preservation by Foster Yeoman's of Merehead; renamed and renumbered Western Yeoman D1035.

Bristol departure. Class 52 No D1007 Western Talisman heads a down express 1B42 out of Temple Meads station about 1970. This was one of the Swindon built machines coming out of works in August 1962 with maroon livery. D1007 was withdrawn in 1974 following an accident at Ealing late in 1973.

DIESEL LOCOMOTIVES : SECOND PHASE

Class	Year first built	Wheel Arrangement	Builder	Horsepower	Engine	Transmission	Max. Speed	No. Built	First BR Numbers
17	1962	Bo-Bo	Clayton Equipt. (88) and Beyer Peacock (29)	900	(2) Paxman 6ZHXL (Note 1)	GEC electric (Note 1)	60	117	D8500–8616
35	1961	B-B	Beyer Peacock	1740	Maybach MD870	Mekydro K184U hydraulic	90	101	D7000–7100
37	1960	Co-Co	English Electric/ Vulcan and R. Stephenson, Hawthorn	1750	English Electric 12CSVT (Note 2)	EE electric	80	309	D6600–6608 D6700–6999
47	1962	Co-Co	Brush and BR Crewe	2750 (Note 3)	Sulzer 12LDA28C (Note 3)	Brush electric	95 (Note 4)	507	D1500–1701 D1707–1999 D1100–1111
48	1965	Co-Co	Brush	2650	Sulzer 12LVA24 (Note 5)	Brush electric	95	5	D1702–1706
52	1961	C-C	BR Swindon and Crewe	2700	(2) Maybach MD655	Voith L630rU hydraulic	90	74	D1000–1073
55	1961	Co-Co	English Electric/Vulcan	3300	(2) Napier Deltic D18/25	EE electric	100	22	D9000–9021

Notes: 1 D8586/7 had two Rolls Royce D engines of same horsepower. Nos D8588–8616 had Crompton Parkinson generators but GEC traction motors.
2 Nos 37901–4 now fitted with Mirrlees MB 275T engines rated at 1800hp, with Brush alternator. Nos 37905–8 now have Ruston RX 270T engines rated at 1800hp, with GEC alternator. Brush and GEC alternators are also fitted to some locomotives now numbered in 374xx, 375xx and 377xx series.
3 Sulzer 12LDA28C engine later downrated to 2580hp. No 47901 (ex D1628) now fitted with Ruston Paxman 12RK3CT engine rated at 3300hp as test bed for class 58.
4 Locomotives in 477xx series geared for 100mph, No 47901 regeared for 80mph.
5 Later re-engined with Sulzer 12LA28C engine to become class 47.

DIESEL LOCOMOTIVES : THIRD PHASE (Electric Train Heating)

Class	Year first built	Wheel Arrangement	Builder	Horsepower	Engine	Transmission	Max. Speed	No. Built	First BR Numbers
50	1967	Co-Co	English Electric/Vulcan	2700	English Electric 16CSVT	EE electric	100	50	D400–449

In addition, earlier locomotives modified to provide electric train heating are class 31 (314xx), class 37 (374xx), class 45 (451xx), class 47 (474xx, 475xx, 476xx and 477xx), in addition to class 33 and the first twenty class 47 equipped from new.

DIESEL LOCOMOTIVES : FOURTH PHASE (Heavy Freight haulage)

Class	Year first built	Wheel Arrangement	Builder	Horsepower	Engine	Transmission	Max. Speed	No. Built	First BR Numbers
56	1976	Co-Co	Electroputerè, Romania (30) and BR Doncaster and Crewe	3250	Ruston Paxman 16RK3CT	Brush electric	80	135	56001– 56135
58	1983	Co-Co	BREL Doncaster	3300	Ruston Paxman 12RK3ACT	Brush electric	80	50	58001– 58050
59	1986	Co-Co	General Motors La Grange, Ill.	3300	Electro Motive Div. 645E3C	EMD electric	60	5	59001– 59005
60	1989	Co-Co	Brush	3100	Mirrlees 8MB275T	Brush electric	80	(Note 6)	60001 onwards

Note: 6 Under construction against initial order for 100 locomotives.

THE DELTICS

Twenty-two names tripped lightly off the tongue of every latter-day railway enthusiast, from the four letter *Meld* to the eight word *The Prince of Wales's Own Regiment of Yorkshire*, eight names of racehorses in the Doncaster tradition, six North Country regiments and eight Scottish regiments from the Border country to the Highlands, which revived some of the army names carried by withdrawn steam locomotives, seven of them ex LMS Royal Scots. It was part of the magic which attached to the class 55s during their working life and lives on in the six which have been preserved.

But names were only part of the magnetism that turned the Deltics into a cult. At 3300hp they were of power not exceeded by any diesel locomotive in the BR fleet, and they set new performance standards on the East Coast main line for fifteen years until displaced by even faster High Speed Trains. Their engine note screamed power, yet their departure from stations was stately, despite the blue cloud of burnt lubricating oil that accompanied it. The high driving position, looking out through gold tinted windscreens gave their drivers the air of supermen.

Certainly the Deltics fascinated Treacy, who set himself the task of photographing every one at work. Even with a knowledge of how the working diagrams would bring them into Leeds it was no mean task for a busy man, and he roamed the East Coast line to complete it.

Durham viaduct with No D9016 Gordon Highlander on the 13.00 Kings Cross–Newcastle in the spring of 1966 or 1967. Two stop signs for extra long trains are visible on the far side of the viaduct indicating where drivers should stop with two or three coaches off the platform.

D9000 Royal Scots Grey heads the Heart of Midlothian, 14.00 Kings Cross–Edinburgh through Hatfield. The date is c1965 as all the BR MkI coaches are still in maroon livery. The train of eleven vehicles includes a 'miniature buffet' fourth from the engine and a restaurant car towards the rear of the train. Note the fine array of upper quadrant semaphore signals and the Great Northern signal box.

No 9001 St Paddy leaves Berwick with the 12.00 Kings Cross– Aberdeen express 1S32 c1970. Although this was the second locomotive to be built it was the first to be delivered by English Electric – to BR Doncaster works early in 1961. By the time this photograph was taken the D prefix had been dropped and the locomotive fitted with dual braking.

D9016 Gordon Highlander being prepared at Leeds Holbeck to haul the 12.30 Leeds–Kings Cross c1970. Behind the locomotive is the demolished roundhouse of the ex Midland shed, which closed to steam on 1 December 1967 signalling the end of steam in the North Eastern Region. Running behind the shed is the viaduct carrying the LNWR's 1882 line from Leeds City through Farnley and Wortley.

The Eastern region had looked at the Modernisation Plan proposals for large locomotives and was not impressed with the 2500hp on offer. The late Gerry Fiennes, Traffic Manager of the Great Northern Line in the late 1950s, was arguing the case for *average* speeds of 75mph to remain competitive with air, and that meant power well in excess of 3000hp. Looking at the prototype Deltic, working on the London Midland region, he liked most of what he saw. It was an expensive locomotive, and maintenance costs would be high, but if it was used intensively those costs could be spread at acceptable levels. When the order was placed in 1958 for twenty two locomotives, plus spares, the cost was nearly £3,500,000. The loan of the prototype Deltic in 1959 for two years confirmed their expectations.

The new locomotives were allocated to Finsbury Park (8), Gateshead (6) and Haymarket (8) and took over the principal day and night services, displacing the Gresley Pacifics to lesser work. As a result 1962 saw the fastest Kings Cross–Edinburgh time brought down to the level six hours. With track realignment and improvement this was further reduced, to 5hrs 50min by 1958 and within a few more years to 5hrs 30min. The locomotives were worked on intensive cyclic diagrams, fuelling and inspections being carried out at any of the three home depots. A five-year contract was negotiated with English Electric whereby the firm provided spares, technical expertise and supervision to guarantee a fleet mileage of 4.5 million miles per annum. When that expired a new contract covered only the repair costs of the Deltic engines. Finally, in 1969 BR took over the whole responsibility.

Serious problems were not slow to develop, and at times it was difficult to keep the locomotives in service in double figures; by 1970/1 the engine overhaul position was being described as 'catastrophic', and there was plenty of trouble with other components, too. There were danger signs that the locomotives were being worked to death, but gradually Doncaster works and the three depots got on top of the situation.

D9002 The King's Own Yorkshire Light Infantry moves out of the old Leeds Central station (now the site of a DIY superstore and Post Office) towards the end of its days in the mid 1960s. The locomotive is now preserved at the National Railway Museum, York.

D9003 Meld stands in Wakefield Westgate station at the head of 1E68 the 17.10 Leeds to Doncaster c1965. The train was an express calling at Wakefield and South Elmsall and although not shown to be worked by a Deltic in the working timetable it appeared to be a regular turn. The loco and possibly the coaches may have formed the 18.25 Doncaster–Kings Cross which was booked for Deltic haulage.

Deltic No D9004 soon to be named Queen's Own Highlander (received on 23 May 1964, note the BR crest has been moved under the number) passes through York with the up Flying Scotsman in 1964. The locomotive carries the winged thistle headboard symbolising the name of the train. D9004 was withdrawn in October 1981 and in common with the other Deltics scrapped, was cut up at Doncaster works.

The introduction of the full HST service in 1979 saw the Deltics largely restricted to overnight trains or diverted to the very tightly timed London–Hull service. But the end was near. The first locomotive was withdrawn at the end of 1980 and cannibalised to keep others running; the numbers dwindled until all were gone by January 1982. Several remain in preservation.

So were they worth all the trauma? *Maybe*, if the management thinking that accepted fixed HST formations had been forthcoming twenty years earlier, the same result might have been achieved at greatly reduced cost with class 47s. It is unlikely, though, that Treacy would have thanked anyone for the suggestion.

Early morning at Kings Cross (08.05 by the station clock) c1970 No 9005 The Prince of Wales's Own Regiment of Yorkshire *is at the head of 1E42 the 23.15 Edinburgh–Kings Cross in platform 10. The stock appears to be BR Mk 1 corridors and sleeping cars.*

171

D9006 in Portobello yard when brand new in the summer of 1961; it did not receive its name The Fife and Forfar Yeomanry until December 1964. There is now a Freightliner depot on this site though it closed in April 1987.

D9007 Pinza takes 1A17, probably for Kings Cross, out of Waverley station Edinburgh around 1969. The locomotive is still in two-tone green but carries a full yellow nose. The horns have been moved from under the buffers as a temporary trial, they were later placed on the top of the nose adjacent to the cab windows on all the members of the class. D9007 has not been fitted with air brake but there is an electric train heating cable above the right hand buffer.

D9008 The Green Howards *stands in platform 9 at York's graceful station sometime in the early 1970s. The engine is in blue livery and is dual fitted. The leading coach too is a modern one for the time a MkIIa BSO carried on B4 type bogies. To the left is a Leeds Holbeck MPD class 45 1Co-Co1 No 24.*

D9009 Alycidon *at Edinburgh Waverley with the up Flying Scotsman c1963. On the left is A.J. Powell one of the authors of this book. The Deltics were originally allocated to three depots Finsbury Park (34G, opened in 1960), Gateshead (52A) and Haymarket (64B). The only other depot to receive the class was York from 1979, as they were replaced on the ECML by HSTs.*

D9010 The King's Own Scottish Borderer *passes Ardsley shed in 1962 whilst heading 1S57 The Queen of Scots Pullman. The engine is as yet unnamed (8 May 1965 at Dumfries) and so the BR crest is still centrally placed on the body sides. On the left alongside the shed wall is A3 Pacific No 60069 Sceptre – which spent its last year at Ardsley before withdrawal in October 1962. There is a J39 behind and a WD 2-8-0 to the right.*

D9011 The Royal Northumberland Fusiliers *leaves Doncaster with the 07.45, 1N03, Kings Cross to Leeds and Bradford c1964. The Doncaster 'Plant' as the works were known is background right with one of the departmental steam shunters, a J50 class 0-6-0 tank on duty. Note that although the through roads are relaid with flat bottom rail the rest is still bullhead.*

The 17.10 Leeds to Doncaster passing Wortley South junction c1965 hauled by D9012 Crepello. The train is on a line which is now electrified and the curve to the left was the direct connection to Bradford. Behind the train is Copley Hill carriage shed serving Leeds Central. The LNWR old line passes underneath the GNR here.

D9013 The Black Watch passes Ardsley North box some five miles short of Leeds with 1N06, an express from Kings Cross, c1965. Note the GNR signal box with its magnificent bargeboards and the mixture of colour-light and semaphore signalling. Other personal services are catered for by a wheel-less box van.

174

Hare Park Junction south east of Wakefield with D9015 Tulyar hauling the 11.34 Bradford to Kings Cross c1966. The line on the right comes in from Crofton West Junction and Wakefield Kirkgate and the train standing at Hare Park's home signal behind a class 40 is a mixed freight.

D9014 The Duke of Wellington's Regiment leaves York on a down express 1A22 sometime in the mid 1960s. The stormy sky with the photographer's skill in pressing the button with the engine's cab under a light patch has made a magnificent diesel picture.

D9016 Gordon Highlander on the
12.30 ex Leeds for Kings Cross
c1970. In 1967 all Leeds traffic was
concentrated on one station on the
site of the old NER/LNWR and
Midland stations allowing the old
and dreadful Leeds Central to be
closed in April. The new station does
not seem to have inspired the
Railway Bishop as this is one of the
few photographs he took of it. On
the left is the site of the old Midland
Wellington station now a parcels
depot. Electrification came in May
1989.

D9017 The Durham Light Infantry
eases the down Yorkshire Pullman
over the points out of platform 10 at
Kings Cross in the summer of 1966.
The train as well as the engine is
new being made up of 1960 built
Metro Cammell Pullman cars
mounted on Commonwealth bogies.
On the left behind class 24 No
D5050, a class 31 leaves York Road
for the Metropolitan Widened Lines.

Kings Cross at 15.50 sometime in the summer of 1970 (the poster on the right hand pillar accurately dates the picture), No 9018 Ballymoss has arrived with the 11.55 Bradford, 12.30 ex Leeds. There is already another Deltic No D9012 at the country end of the train so this stock probably formed the 16.05 back to Bradford.

D9019 Royal Highland Fusilier at the head of 1A16, the down Flying Scotsman composed of Mk1 stock plus one Thompson coach, passing Craigentinny around 1964. Derby built class 4MT 2-6-4 tank No 80006 waits at the yard signal with a train of empty stock.

D9020 Nimbus sets out from platform 8 at Kings Cross with 1S42, the 16.00 summer train for Edinburgh in 1970. The locomotive is in blue livery with a full yellow nose but the prefix has not yet been dropped. The lettering under the BR logo is D9020's allocation number 34G, Finsbury Park.

D9021 Argyll & Sutherland Highlander, *the last Deltic to be introduced, heads north through Doncaster with 1A30 The Heart of Midlothian a Kings Cross–Edinburgh service in the mid 1960s. There is an inspection saloon in the bay platform to the right.*

DELTIC CHRONOLOGY

numbers first	TOPS	name	to traffic	first depot	withdrawn
D9000	55022	Royal Scots Grey	2/1961	64B	1/1982*
D9001	55001	St. Paddy	2/1961	34G	1/1980
D9002	55002	The King's Own Yorkshire Light Infantry	3/1961	52A	1/1982*
D9003	55003	Meld	3/1961	34G	12/1980
D9004	55004	Queen's Own Highlander	5/1961	64B	10/1981
D9005	55005	The Prince of Wales's Own Regiment of Yorkshire	5/1961	52A	2/1981
D9006	55006	The Fife and Forfar Yeomanry	6/1961	64B	2/1981
D9007	55007	Pinza	6/1961	34G	12/1981
D9008	55008	The Green Howards	7/1961	52A	12/1981
D9009	55009	Alycidon	7/1961	34G	1/1982*
D9010	55010	The King's Own Scottish Borderer	7/1961	64B	11/1981
D9011	55011	The Royal Northumberland Fusiliers	8/1961	52A	11/1981
D9012	55012	Crepello	9/1961	34G	5/1981
D9013	55013	The Black Watch	9/1961	64B	12/1981
D9014	55014	The Duke of Wellington's Regiment	9/1961	52A	11/1981
D9015	55015	Tulyar	10/1961	34G	1/1982*
D9016	55016	Gordon Highlander	10/1961	64B	12/1981*
D9017	55017	The Durham Light Infantry	11/1961	52A	12/1981
D9018	55018	Ballymoss	11/1961	34G	10/1981
D9019	55019	Royal Highland Fusilier	12/1961	64B	12/1981*
D9020	55020	Nimbus	2/1962	34G	1/1980
D9021	55021	Argyll and Sutherland Highlander	5/1962	64B	12/1981

depot codes
34G Finsbury Park
52A Gateshead
64B Haymarket

*   Locomotive now preserved

ELECTRIC LOCOMOTIVES

In spite of the electrification carried out by three of the companies and their constituents, British Railways in 1948 inherited just fourteen electric locomotives (excluding battery locomotives and suchlike oddities). There were two modern Southern Co-Co 'Boosters' for 660v with third rail, with another planned, and one LNER Bo-Bo 1500v prototype for the Manchester–Sheffield–Wath electrification deferred by World War II; at the time it was on loan to the Netherlands Railways. The remainder was an elderly ragbag. It was not exactly a treasure trove.

Until 1937 the Southern Railway had been happy as an electric multiple unit line, since freight was a minority source of revenue. But then Oliver Bulleid and Alfred Raworth (Electrical Engineer) got together to produce a scheme for a mixed traffic electric locomotive. There were two interesting features; the use of two booster generator sets incorporating heavy flywheels to take it through gaps in the conductor rail when no collector shoes were in contact, and a light roof

LNER/Metropolitan Vickers designed class EM1 1500v dc Bo-Bo electric No 26052 (later 76052) waits with an up GC section express at Manchester London Road in 1955. The station was renamed Piccadilly in September 1960. The Woodhead route closed to passenger traffic in 1970 and completely in July 1981, although the route to Hadfield and Glossop remains open using the standard 25kv overhead wires. On the right is a GCR matchboard side coach amazingly still in service.

pantograph for working in yards and depots from simple overhead catenary where a third rail would be a hazard to shunters and others. Three were built (see Table 00) to a very plain body design.

Only the Central and Western sections of the Southern were able to use the 'Boosters', and so they ran overnight freight trains from Norwood or New Cross yards to Portsmouth and to Polegate, near Eastbourne. They were always allocated to Stewarts Lane depot. After the war they took over the Newhaven boat trains running to and from Victoria, a preserve they held until 1964, when they transferred to a Portsmouth–Brighton passenger working. None of this was within Treacy's orbit, and they were withdrawn in 1968/9, superseded by more modern designs.

By June 1959 the first stage of the Kent Coast electrification was in service (Ramsgate, and Dover Marine via Canterbury) giving considerable scope for locomotive haulage of boat trains and trains of ferry vans. In readiness an order was placed for a new fleet of twenty five electric locomotives, which became class 71 and also went to Stewarts Lane depot. They differed from their three predecessors in being of Bo-Bo arrangement and were very much lighter. The traction motors were carried on the bogie frames, with flexible drives; they had a one hour rating of 2550hp. The 71s had a single booster generator set and shunting pantograph. The boxy look of the original three gave way to slightly curved sides, a gently sloping front end with rounded corners, and windscreens which had a curious 'raised eyebrows' look.

The greater part of their work was during the dark hours, including the Night Ferry. From mid 1961 they also took over the prestige

A 1500v dc class EM2 Co-Co electric locomotive No 27004 leaves London Road with a Manchester–Marylebone train, which it worked as far as Sheffield, soon after the completion of electrification in 1954. The locomotive is in its original black livery with red lining. It was later painted green and named Juno *in 1959. The seven EM2s were put into store at Bury in 1968 and subsequently sold to Nederlandse Spoorwegen – No 27004 became NS 1503.*

Class 81 3200hp Bo-Bo No E3010, allocated to Glasgow Shields Road, approaches Beattock on an up fitted express freight in 1974 not long after the completion of the WCML 25kv electrification. The stub of the one time Moffat branch can be seen on the right. Another sign of the times is the lack of a brake van at the rear of the train.

Modern trains come to Liverpool Lime Street. Class AL5 25kv electric locomotives Nos E3057 and E3056 stand awaiting their next turns of duty c1967–8. The photograph shows opposite sides of the locomotives which were both 1961 Doncaster built machines.

*Class 85 No 85032 heads a
northbound mineral train down
from Shap c1976. These locomotives
originally carried two pantographs
but one was later removed and air
reservoirs fitted in its place. Train
reporting numbers on route
indicator panels were abandoned in
the mid 1970s which helps to date
this picture.*

Golden Arrow service and, for a time, the Newhaven workings. This was work on which they did not cross Treacy's path. But being tied to the third rail made their full utilisation difficult, particularly in the freight field.

The idea of a dual power locomotive, electric with either diesel or battery supplementary power, had circulated on the Southern Railway since the 1930s, but was put on ice when the booster electrics were planned. The idea was reactivated in 1956; by 1959 an order was placed for six Bo-Bo locomotives to the restricted Hastings line gauge and in the same power bracket electrically as the class 33 Cromptons, but fitted with a 600hp English Electric diesel engine as used on the Hampshire demus. They became class 73, and were the first electro-diesel locomotives in the world.

Compared with the 71s they were straight sided and with a more matter of fact front end treatment. Simple nose-suspended motors were used, and there was no booster generator set, since the diesel engine could be brought into use in the event of the locomotive becoming 'gapped'. The control gear was carefully arranged so that they could multiple with emu stock and with motor luggage vans.

Based on Stewarts Lane depot, they were put to work on freight and van trains worked from Hither Green, and on transfer freights between there and Feltham. So successful and versatile did they prove that further orders were soon placed for another forty-three locomotives which constituted subclass 73/1. While broadly similar to the earlier six, the bogies were to a new design which seemed to make them more prone to slipping.

Their initial allocation was to Stewarts Lane, though in later years they wandered somewhat. They turned up all over the Southern region on freight and special passenger workings, even on Royal trains. Undoubtedly one of the most interesting duties began in 1984, when they inaugurated the new regular interval 'Gatwick Express' service on a push/pull basis, with the locomotive at the country end of an eight coach train with a converted driving luggage van at the other.

The arrival of the class 73s, and traffic changes which included the rundown of wagon load freight, resulted in ten class 71 electrics being considered redundant, while at the same time there was an unsatisfied demand for the versatile electro-diesels. This led to the conversion of ten class 71s into class 74 machines. Weight limitations would not permit use of the same English Electric diesel engine, and a lightweight Paxman unit was used instead. New body sides were necessary, but the original cabs were reused; the pantographs were removed. The control system involved one of the first applications of thyristors in rail traction. They were allocated to Eastleigh depot, working over a Bournemouth line and into Southampton Docks, and beyond the third rail to Poole, including some work in multiple with electric multiple units.

The class 74s, with their modern features, *should* have been most valuable machines; in practice they proved a near disaster. They quickly established a reputation for failures, there were engine starting problems, the electronic system was not suited to the traction environment, and bogie modifications had spoiled the riding quality. They had to be kept off the more taxing work, and enginemen had no confidence in them. They were withdrawn by 1977.

*A class 86 Bo-Bo No E3167
approaches Stockport Edgeley
station (renamed Stockport in 1968)
over the well known brick viaduct in
the late 1960s. The stock, in the new
blue and grey livery, is a mixture of
MkI and MkII coaches. This was an
exciting moment as the full electric
service between Manchester and
London began in April 1966.*

182

Class 87 Bo-Bo No 87022 takes an express over the northern approaches to Shap Summit c1975. The stock is a mixture of Mk1, II and III coaches. No 87022 carries its original crossed arm pantograph and was named Cock o' the North *in 1978, the year of Eric Treacy's death.*

Away from the Southern region, official policy followed the recommendation of the 1927 Pringle Committee, that new electrification schemes should use 1500v dc with overhead conductor. In 1935 the LNER, backed by cheap government money, had authorised the first main line electrification in Britain on this system, from Manchester via Woodhead to Sheffield and Wath. The scheme made provision for seventy Bo-Bo locomotives to handle both passenger and freight. World War II put an end to progress, but Doncaster works produced a prototype locomotive with regenerative braking which ran limited trials on the Manchester South Junction and Altrincham line before being stored 'for the duration'. An interesting feature was the mounting of buffers and drawgear on the bogies, which were articulated by a linkage. After the war it was loaned to the Netherlands Railways to assist in their rehabilitation and to get early feedback on its performance. This soon showed that the riding was very rough at speed, and some bogie redesign was undertaken.

After British Railways took over responsibility for the resumed scheme (now pared down to sixty five locomotives) R.A. Riddles was not convinced that these locomotives, which became class 76, would ever give a satisfactory ride in express passenger service, and so the last seven were built to a new Co-Co design, using an adaptation of the splendid bogies used under the LMS diesels Nos 10000/1 and with buffers and drawgear transferred to the underframe. Neither design was a thing of beauty. The body was all panels and riveted butt strips, smothered in ventilation grilles and windows, while the cabs, with almost flat roofs, square windscreens and oddly shaped side windows, looked distinctly crude. Treacy seemed to feel under an obligation to

184

photograph them without wasting any time in doing so. An outing to Manchester London Road was sufficient.

The old Great Central route to London was doomed, however. First the electrified West Coast line eroded its through traffic; the class 77s were put into store in 1968 and sold to the Netherlands the following year, just before the through passenger trains ceased. Then the rundown of the coal industry enabled the coal flows to be rationalised away from the high-cost route from Wath via Woodhead, and the line was closed between Penistone and Hadfield in 1981, consigning the class 76s to the torch.

But even as the MSW scheme was becoming visible in masts and catenary, events were moving on. In France the pioneering work on the use of ac current at industrial frequency was demonstrating the superiority of 25kV ac over 1500v dc for main lines. The trial re-equipment of the Lancaster–Morecambe–Heysham line on this system in 1953, provided BR with valuable experience of new line and on-train equipment. Thus in 1955, when the decision was taken to electrify the West Coast main line from Manchester, Liverpool and Birmingham to Euston, there was no doubt in BR that 25kV 50Hz was the system to adopt on performance and economic grounds.

This network came into service progressively from 1960 until completion in 1967. It was a remarkable achievement carried out under heavy traffic – though at times the disruption to the service was considerable. To operate it, one hundred locomotives of five designs

With some brand new MkIII coaches at the head of its train class 86 Bo-Bo electric No 86206 (originally E3184 and named City of Stoke on Trent in 1978) climbs to Shap near Greenholme c1975. Two interesting points come to light on close inspection. Note the different bogies with Flexicoil suspension compared to those on E3167 at Stockport and the fact that Eric Treacy has misjudged the speed of the train – the shutter has not quite stopped the front of the engine. It was difficult in those early days of electrification to appreciate the vast difference in power of the electrics and their virtual ignorance of such gradients as Shap.

were ordered, subsequently redesignated classes 81–85; all met a common specification for a Bo-Bo locomotive with driving cabs at each end, not exceeding 80 tons, and exerting about 3300hp (one hour rating) to enable them to haul passenger trains of 475 tons at 90mph or 950 ton freight trains at 55mph on the level. It was originally intended that two of the classes would have some examples geared for 100mph and others for 80mph for freight haulage, but this idea was dropped at the last minute. Only two were actually built geared for freight work, and they were soon altered to standard. In addition forty five four car electric multiple units (class 304) were ordered for work in the Liverpool/Manchester area, with a further order later for fifty emus of improved design (class 310) for work out of Euston.

The first four locomotive types, which became classes 81, 82, 83 and 84 were mechanical variations on a common theme. They all used mercury arc rectifiers to convert ac current to the dc used by the traction motors, because at the time solid state rectifiers had not been reliability-proved in traction service. In addition the traction motors were mounted on the bogie frames to keep down unsprung weight and thus damage to the track. The table on page 191 sets out the details. Class 85 took the plunge with silicon and germanium rectifiers, being slightly later than the other four, and also used frame mounted motors.

Quiet strength. A photograph which must have evoked memories of happy days at Lime Street and Edge Hill when the scene would not have been as quiet as this. Class AL6 No E3185 (now 86405) waits noiselessly for the right away before gliding up the 1 in 93 gradient though the steep smoke begrimed cutting to Edge Hill. The date would be around 1971.

It was not long before the rectifiers on classes 81–84 were in trouble and causing serious unreliability. By 1966 all the 83s were in store at Bury while management pondered what to do; a year later all the 84s joined them. The 85s were doing the lion's share of the hardest work with the others partly relegated to parcels and other slower trains. Only the arrival of the new class 86 locomotives saved the day. Nor were the problems all electrical, for 100mph running soon showed up the mechanical weaknesses. The 81s, 83s and 84s were notoriously rough riders, in contrast to the 82s, which rode quite smoothly. In the early 1970s all were put through Crewe works for major refurbishment which included fitting new silicon rectifiers. But mechanical problems persisted, and all of classes 82, 83 and 84 were withdrawn after a relatively short active life; the 84s were the first to go, by 1979, the 82s four years later and the last two 83s in 1989 after being confined to Euston empty carriage workings for some years. At the beginning of 1989 there were just eleven 81s left, and their retention will be brief. Some of these early ac locomotive classes are thinly represented among

Crewe c1971. Train No 1A51 the 13.22 Liverpool–Euston via Birmingham leaves behind 3600hp Bo-Bo electric Class AL6/86 No E3103. The engine is in rail blue livery with aluminium emblem and numbers. Note the pre 1985 track layout and the PW staff now with high visibility jackets. Much of the original LNWR station is still intact including the wind screens although platforms west of the present No 12 are no longer in use.

187

Treacy's photographs, but in view of their lengthy periods either in store or in works this is not surprising. Among the changes made, one at least would have been visible to him, the removal of the second pantographs in the 1970s.

If BR began to wonder what they had let themselves in for with these first four classes, the class 85 must have done much to restore faith in ac electrification. Rough riders they may have been – though this was retrospectively improved by fitting additional dampers – but they were all fitted with solid state rectifiers which were reliable, and they also introduced rheostatic braking to the West Coast main line. They have proved a valuable backup to the younger front line locomotives, though at slack times they have been stored in considerable numbers. A few have been withdrawn as a result of damage, but Treacy recorded them all over the system, in Euston and Lime Street on passenger work and in the Cumbrian fells on freight.

In readiness for completion of electrification to Euston in April 1966 (Birmingham and Stoke were not brought in until March 1967) orders were placed for one hundred second generation Bo-Bo locomotives. The success of the rectifiers and traction equipment on the class 85s made it relatively straightforward to build on this foundation. Unfortunately, one fundamentally wrong decision was taken at this time in the interests of economy which has bedevilled the class 86 ever since; nose-suspended motors were used instead of the earlier frame-borne type. The official view was that 'special designs incorporating full suspension are an unnecessary expense', but probably within ten years the speaker would willingly have eaten his words!

The class 86s have proved much more reliable than any of their predecessors, but the class soon established a reputation for rough riding, particularly through points and crossings. Running for much of their time at 100mph, with smaller diameter wheels and high unsprung weight of their traction motors, the 86s not only caused serious track damage and broken rails but the locomotive equipment began to suffer, too. Three of them were fitted with new bogies with frame-borne motors as guineapigs for the later class 87, but this modification was too expensive to make to them all. The riding problem was attacked by designing a new bogie with modified secondary suspension in the form of nests of three Flexicoil springs, with their own dampers, to support the body from each bogie. To minimise the track damage most of the 86s have also been fitted with the Swedish SAB resilient wheel; initial trials at 100mph showed a fifty per cent drop in vertical dynamic forces at track irregularities.

Differing combinations of these two modifications have given rise to a confusing and seemingly never-ending series of renumberings, and in addition some have been regeared for a maximum speed of 75mph and restricted to freight work. The current subdivision of the class is summarised in a footnote to the table on p191.

Only one other ac locomotive class emerged during Treacy's lifetime, comprising thirty six class 87 Bo-Bos developed from the class 86 but of greater power and with fully suspended traction motors. The last one to be built, No 87101, differs from its sisters in having thyristor control; for a long time it was regarded as experimental because of possible interference with signalling and telecommunications circuits.

The 87s proved also to be rough riding, though this has been tamed by modifications to the bogies. It has not been practicable to improve their proneness to 'lose their feet' when rail adhesion conditions are bad, and as a result the original specified loads over Shap and Beattock proved impracticable. This has necessitated fitting for multiple working on heavy Anglo-Scottish freight trains, mainly Freightliner. Discussions on a Co-Co machine for such duties, in the class 89 mould, are as yet inconclusive.

Lastly, the rakish looking class 90s on the West Coast and class 91s on the Kings Cross–Leeds trains are in service. How Treacy would have revelled in the picture opportunities they offered while rueing the missed opportunities given by now extinct classes. His ac locomotive pictures span the period from the four-digit headcodes until their demise in noughts and spots in the 1970s, but not into the marker lights and headlight era. The coaches to which they are attached cover the whole range from Mark Is to the sleek and silent Mark IIIs, but in maroon, BR blue and grey, or Pullman silver; not for Treacy the kaleidoscopic liveries of today. Had he lived on, he would have been hard pressed to record the accelerating pace of change.

Euston in the early days of electrification with class AL6 Bo-Bo No E3200 after arrival at the terminus around 1966–7. The locomotive was built by English Electric at Vulcan Foundry in 1966 and after three renumberings became 86429 in 1985 carrying the name The Times. On 19 September 1986 No 86429 was in collision with No 86211 at Colwich Junction Staffordshire and so severely damaged that it was eventually scrapped. These are early times, for the station roof has not yet been completed.

NO ENTRY FOR PASSENGERS

DC ELECTRIC LOCOMOTIVES

BR Class	Year first built	Wheel Arrgt.	Voltage and current collection	Builder	Electrical Equipment	Horse-power	Max. Speed	No. Built	First BR Numbers
–	1904	Bo-Bo	600 3rd rail & o/h	Brush, Loughborough	BTH nose suspended motors and electrical equipment.	640	25	2	26500/1
–	1914	Bo-Bo	1500 o/h	NER Darlington	EE nose suspended motors, Siemens electrical equipment	1100	45	10	26502–11
–	1922	2-Co-2	1500 o/h	NER Darlington	Metro-Vick frame mounted motors, quill drive	1800	20	1	26600
70	1941	Co-Co	660 3rd rail & o/h	BR Ashford	EE nose suspended motors, twin booster sets	1470	75	2	20001–3
71	1959	Bo-Bo	660 3rd rail & o/h	BR Doncaster	EE frame-mounted motors with Brown Boveri flexible drive single booster set	2550	90	25	E5000–5024
76	1941	Bo-Bo	1500 o/h	BR Gorton	Metro-Vick, nose-suspended motors, regenerative braking	1868	65	58	26000–26057
77	1954	Co-Co	1500 o/h	BR Gorton	Metro-Vick, nose-suspended motors, regenerative braking	2490	90	7	27000–27006

ELECTRO-DIESEL LOCOMOTIVES

BR Class	Year first built	Wheel Arrgt.	Voltage and current collection	Builder	Electrical Equipment	Horse-power	Max. Speed	No. Built	First BR Numbers
73	1962	Bo-Bo	750	BR Eastleigh	EE nose suspended motors	1600 (1 hour)	80	6	E6001–6006
					EE 4SRKT diesel engine	600			
73/1	1965	Bo-Bo	750	English Electric/Vulcan F.	EE nose suspended motors	1600 (1 hour)	90	43	E6007–6049
					EE 4SRKT diesel engine	600			
74	1967 (Note 1)	Bo-Bo	750	BR Crewe	EE nose suspended motors	2500 (1 hour)	75	10	E6101–6110
					Paxman 6YJXL diesel engine Single booster set	650			

Notes: 1 Rebuilt from redundant class 71 electric locomotives.

Crewe station around 1967 with English Electric class AL3 (class 83) No E3025 and a new class 86 waiting on the middle roads. All the station signs are in the early BR style red enamel with white lettering.

25kV AC ELECTRIC LOCOMOTIVES

BR Class	Year first built	Wheel Arrgt.	Builder	Electrical Equipment	Continuous Rating hp	Max. Speed mph	No. Built	First BR Numbers
81	1959	Bo-Bo	Birmingham RC&W	AEI Rugby: Mercury arc rectifiers, tap changer control, bogie frame mounted motors, Alsthom quill drive.	3200	100	25	E3001–3023 E3096/7
82	1960	Bo-Bo	Beyer Peacock	AEI Manchester: Mercury arc rectifiers, tap changer control, bogie frame mounted motors, Alsthom quill drive.	3300	100	10	E3046–3055
83	1960	Bo-Bo	English Electric/Vulcan Fdy.	EE: Mercury arc rectifiers, tap changer control, bogie frame mounted motors, SLM resilient drive (Note 1)	2950	100	13	E3024–3035 E3100
						80 (Note 2)	2	E3303/4 (Note 2)
84	1960	Bo-Bo	North British Loco	GEC: Mercury arc rectifiers, tap changer control, bogie frame mounted motors, SLM flexible drive.	3100	100	10	E3036–3045
85	1960	Bo-Bo	BR Doncaster	AEI Rugby: Germanium (30) and Silicon (10) rectifiers, tap changer control, bogie frame mounted motors, Alsthom quill drive, rheostatic brake.	3200	100	40	E3056–3095
86 (Note 3)	1965	Bo-Bo	BR Doncaster (40) English Electric/Vulcan Fdy (60)	EE: Transformers, silicon rectifiers, etc. AEI: Nose suspended motors, etc. Tap changer control, rheostatic brake.	3600	100 (Note 3)	100	E3101–3200
87	1973	Bo-Bo	BR Crewe	GEC Traction: Silicon rectifiers, tap changer control, bogie frame mounted motors, flexible shaft drive, rheostatic brake. (Note 4)	5000	110 (Note 4)	35	87001–87035 87101
89	1986	Co-Co	BREL Crewe	Brush	5850	125	1	89001
90	1987	Bo-Bo	BREL Crewe	GEC Traction: Thyristor converters, microprocessor control, bogie frame mounted motors, flexible shaft drive, push-pull fitted, rheostatic brake.	5000	110	50 (Note 5)	90001–90050
91	1988	Bo-Bo	BREL Crewe	GEC Traction: Thyristor converters, microprocessor control, body mounted motors with shaft drive, push-pull fitted, rheostatic brake.	6085	125	31 (Note 5)	91001–91031

Notes: 1 Last locomotive (E3304) fitted with prototype silicon rectifier.
2 Two locomotives geared for 80mph when built, but quickly converted to standard and renumbered E3098/9.
3 Class 86 is now all fitted with Flexicoil suspension and subdivided as follows:-

Subclass	No	Owning Sector	Wheels	Special Fittings	Continuous hp	Max. Speed
86/1	3	InterCity	Monobloc	Class 87 bogies and motors	5000	110
86/2	59	InterCity	SAB resilient		4040	100
86/4	28	InterCity, Parcels, Freight	SAB resilient		4040	100
86/6	10	Freight	Monobloc		4040	75

4 One locomotive subclassed 87/1, with thyristor control and push-pull fitted. Max speed 100mph.
5 Classes 90 and 91 still being produced.

The down Royal Scot leaves Euston for Glasgow Central around 1966–7. The train make up and livery is very much a sign of the times, the blue and grey livery has just come into service whilst the mostly maroon painted stock carries destination boards with a tartan background as does the gangway door to Swindon built BFK M14013. The spotter on the left clutching a railway magazine will have just copped No E3179 at the head of the train.